1st Workshop on Teaching for NLP (Teach4NLP 2023)

Ingolstadt, Germany
18 September 2023

ISBN: 979-8-3313-1648-8

Printed from e-media with permission by:

Curran Associates, Inc.
57 Morehouse Lane
Red Hook, NY 12571

proceedings.com

Some format issues inherent in the e-media version may also appear in this print version.

Association for Computational Linguistics
209 N. Eighth Street
Stroudsburg, Pennsylvania 18360

Phone: 1-570-476-8006
Fax: 1-570-476-0860

acl@aclweb.org

Additional copies of this publication are available from:

Curran Associates, Inc.
57 Morehouse Lane
Red Hook, NY 12571 USA
Phone: 845-758-0400
Fax: 845-758-2633
Email: curran@proceedings.com
Web: www.proceedings.com

Teach4NLP 2023

The 1st Workshop on Teaching for NLP

Proceedings of the Workshop

September 18, 2023

Order copies of this and other ACL proceedings from:

Association for Computational Linguistics (ACL)
209 N. Eighth Street
Stroudsburg, PA 18360
USA
Tel: +1-570-476-8006
Fax: +1-570-476-0860
acl@aclweb.org

Introduction

These proceedings are a collection of the papers presented at the KONVENS Teaching for NLP (Teach4NLP) Workshop in Ingolstadt, Bavaria, Germany, on September 18, 2023. Teaching Natural Language Processing (NLP) and Computational Linguistics (CL) has always been complex and challenging due to the many facets and sub-areas involved in these highly interdisciplinary subjects. In recent years, this challenge has further intensified as a result of the rapid technical advancements these fields have undergone (e. g., the advent of large generative language models capable of generating human-like texts). The rapid pace of this progress has not only massively increased the awareness of NLP and CL among the general public, but also poses a number of salient questions from an educational point of view, including the following:

- Have recent advancements made other, more "traditional" NLP techniques obsolete, meaning that they should be dropped from our curricula? If so, which ones? For example, does the dominance of transformer models mean that recurrent neural networks do not have to be taught anymore?
- Out of the currently emerging methods and technologies, which ones will turn out to be "fads" and which ones will stand the test of time – and thus should be included in a curriculum? For example, should NLP educators today take the time to explain Reinforcement Learning from Human Feedback (RLHF) in detail?
- Does the growing number of easy to use, off-the-shelf NLP tools reduce the need to know about specific technical details of NLP pipelines (e. g., what a tokenizer is and why one is needed)? In relation to this, is our focus mainly on teaching the next generation of researchers, or rather expert users of NLP systems?
- Many state-of-the-art systems today are trained in a purely end-to-end fashion and rely very little (if at all) on linguistic concepts and abstractions. Does this mean that NLP curricula should spend less time and effort on teaching these linguistic ideas?

Apart from these "technical" questions, there are also many arising issues relating to the ethical and societal implications of working with language technology that need to be addressed in teaching. For example, how can we ensure that our models do not reproduce harmful stereotypes, or that they respect the privacy of their users? How can we properly address the need for systems and data in less-resourced languages – or even any language other than English?

Finally, due to the increasing prominence of NLP and CL in recent years, student populations in our courses are becoming increasingly heterogeneous: Students may come from different social and cultural backgrounds, may study a range of subjects at different levels of experience, and may be interested in different application scenarios. How can we design courses and teaching materials that best cater to such diverse audiences? More specifically, how can we best accommodate students who have little to no technical experience, and how is it possible to motivate those students who feel that their teacher's answers to these questions may be inadequate?

All of these issues can feel overwhelming even to experienced teachers, and more so to newcomers to our field. As a result, we were motivated to organize a workshop that allows us to exchange experiences, best practices, and suggestions for how best to teach NLP and CL in various settings and address the challenges described above (as well as many others not mentioned here). In addition, being co-located with KONVENS, a secondary motivation was to bring together educators who are either involved in the German academic system, are teaching to German-speaking audiences in other contexts, or are dealing with the German language as part of their curricula. Our hope is that our meeting can serve as one step towards building a collection of resources and a community that offers mutual support in questions of teaching and exchange ideas on how to tackle the challenges we face when teaching NLP.

The Workshop Organizers:
Annemarie Friedrich, Stefan Grünewald, Margot Mieskes, Jannik Strötgen, Christian Wartena

Organizing Committee

Organizers

Annemarie Friedrich, Augsburg University

Stefan Grünewald, Bosch Center for Artificial Intelligence

Margot Mieskes, Darmstadt University of Applied Sciences

Jannik Strötgen, Karlsruhe University of Applied Sciences

Christian Wartena, Hannover University of Applied Sciences and Arts

Program Committee

Program Committee

Heike Adel, Stuttgart Media University

Anette Frank, Heidelberg University

Annemarie Friedrich, Augsburg University

Stefan Grünewald, Bosch Center for Artificial Intelligence

Cerstin Mahlow, Zurich University of Applied Sciences

Margot Mieskes, Darmstadt University of Applied Sciences

Ulrike Padó, Stuttgart Technology University of Applied Sciences

Barbara Plank, IT University of Copenhagen

Jakob Prange, Hong Kong Polytechnic University

Nils Reiter, Cologne University

Ines Rehbein, Mannheim University

Jannik Strötgen, Karlsruhe University of Applied Sciences

Christian Wartena, Hannover University of Applied Sciences and Arts

Alessandra Zarcone, Augsburg Technical University of Applied Sciences

Torsten Zesch, Hagen University

Table of Contents

Conference Program

Monday, September 18, 2023

13:00–13:45 ***Welcome & Introduction***

13:45–15:30 ***Discussion: Designing NLP curricula***

15:30–16:30 ***Coffee break & Poster session***

Including a contemporary NLP application within an introductory course: an example with student feedback from a University of Applied Sciences
Saurabh Kumar and Alessandra Zarcone

Democratizing Machine Learning for Interdisciplinary Scholars: Reflections on the NLP+CSS Tutorial Series
Ian Stewart and Katherine Keith

Working at your own Pace: Computer-based Learning for CL
Anselm Knebusch and Ulrike Padó

QUEST: Quizzes Utilizing Engaging StoryTelling
Thomas Arnold

An educational Gamebook on computational linguistic methods for the development of taxonomies
Fritz Kliche, Ulrich Heid, Ralf Knackstedt and Thomas Klupp

16:30–17:45 ***Breakout discussion groups***

Examples & visualization

Teaching with limited resources

Assessments & exams

Monday, September 18, 2023 (continued)

Scaling & activation

17:45–18:00 ***Wrap-up***

Including a contemporary NLP application within an introductory course: an example with student feedback from a University of Applied Sciences

Saurabh Kumar
Artificial Intelligence Technologies
FORVIA Clean Mobility
Augsburg, Germany
saurabh.kumar@forvia.com

Alessandra Zarcone
Technische Hochschule Augsburg
Fakultät für Informatik
Augsburg, Germany
alessandra.zarcone@hs-augsburg.de

Abstract

The recent extensive media coverage of Large Language Models and their applications like ChatGPT have created an unprecedented awareness and curiosity related to Natural Language Processing (NLP) amongst university students from different fields. However, students must understand and master a number of theoretical topics before they can understand how such models work and how they are applied to real-life examples. Within an introductory NLP course at a University of Applied Sciences, we asked ourselves how to best include teaching material related to contemporary applications in order to encourage students to experiment on their own, not only within the course but also later in their studies or in an industrial setting. What could be the major components and how could it be made accessible for students from different programs? What would be the added value compared to a plethora of existing online videos and tutorials? We present our experience with a step-by-step session on a contemporary applied topic, namely Semantic Textual Similarity. We share the examples, the visualization, the slides and the code samples used in the session. We discuss the students' feedback as well as further possibilities for similar future sessions.

1 Introduction

The extensive debates in the media and the publicity received by Large Language Models (LLMs) like GPT4 (OpenAI, 2023) and LaMDA (Thoppilan et al., 2022) that power dialogue-based applications like ChatGPT and Bard respectively has led to heightened curiosity about Natural Language Processing amongst university students. This is particularly the case for students at University of Applied Sciences (*Hochschulen* in the German system), who focus more on use-case-oriented applied research and are fascinated by the industrial applications of NLP and in particular of LLMs, as well as of dialog or assistance systems.

This focus on industrial applications makes it worthwhile to provide students at Universities of Applied Sciences tools to better understand these technologies, their capabilities and their shortcomings as well as opportunities to come up with their own use cases. However, this could constitute a challenge in introductory courses, as students must first understand a number of basic concepts and have the possibility to work with some realistic data, before being able to explore the possibilities and limitations of the most recent approaches. It is thus not trivial to choose a contemporary topic that can be used to explain basic theoretical concepts while being relevant for many practical applications at the same time. Additionally, there are constraints related to required computational power and ease of creating own data.

We chose the topic of Semantic Textual Similarity (STS, Agirre et al., 2012) to introduce the challenges of sentence embeddings as well as their relevance for real-world use cases. We present our experience, provide the materials. We include the feedback provided by the students and discuss the possibilities to further improve selection of topics, and measure student pro-activeness in using the provided code for their own experiments.

2 The Introductory NLP Course

The course, held at the Technische Hochschule Augsburg, consists of 12 units. Each unit consists of four consecutive 45 minute slots, with a short break after the first two. The teaching slots are organized with an alternation of frontal teaching with slides and practical exercises using jupyter notebooks and student presentations. During the current semester (summer semester 2023), 44 students from the Bachelor programs *Informatik*, *Wirtschaftsinformatik* and *Interaktive Medien* and from the Master programs *Informatik, Business Information Systems* and *Applied Research* enrolled in the course, choosing it as one of their electives.

Proceedings of the 1st Workshop on Teaching for NLP, pages 1–7
September 18, 2023. ©2023 Association for Computational Linguistics

The Master students as well as the students of *Interaktive Medien* are required to integrate their written exam with either a presentation during class, or a report on relevant papers, or a report on a small, practical project.

The topics of the first 10 units roughly correspond to the content and materials in Chapters 2 to 11 of Jurafsky and Martin (2023), while the last two units are dedicated to Chatbots and Dialogue Systems (Chapter 15).

3 Choosing a contemporary application

Our aim was to introduce a contemporary application in the middle of the course, with the goal of making the significance of some basic, already-introduced theoretical concepts evident and of increasing the students' curiosity about the topics which would be introduced later in the course. We wanted to introduce a topic where the students themselves could explore the effectiveness and shortcomings of simple methods and follow it up with exploration of newer methods and under what conditions they would be useful. We thus picked the topic of Semantic Textual Similarity (STS), with a focus on popular semantic information retrieval systems that combine sentence embeddings (Reimers and Gurevych, 2019) and vector indices (Johnson et al., 2021) with existing methods like BM25 (Robertson and Zaragoza, 2009). The unit on Semantic Textual Similarity was presented during Unit 6, that is after the introducing language modeling (n-grams), text classification (Naïve Bayes and logistic regression) and vector semantics (word embeddings) in the previous units. During the same unit, feedforward networks were introduced as models for language modeling and textual classification. We introduced the limitation of their input to a fixed-length word window and the question of how word-level embeddings can be best combined to represent word sequences (for example, in order to represent a document to be categorized). Our goal was to make the students aware of the fact that they could think of extending the code samples provided in the session to achieve information retrieval quality similar to some of the state-of-the-art systems. The code and slides are available in the GitHub repository at: `https://github.com/saurabhkumar/lecture1_semantic_similarity`.

4 Datasets, result visualization and computational needs

It is common practice to request students to download standard datasets from the internet and work with it in the courses. This has the advantage that datasets can be reused, and the course material can be standardized. However, students from Universities of Applied Sciences may be more interested in use-case specific datasets than in standard benchmarks. Furthermore, it is also challenging in an introductory course to make students understand why algorithm performance on a benchmark dataset does not always translate to good performance on their own real-word examples and what characteristics of their example data are not covered in the benchmark dataset.

To overcome this limitation, we created a small set of examples at increasing levels of complexity, based on the contrast of different general-domain concepts such as countries, capitals, language, economics, demographics, and cuisine. The data can be obtained from Wikipedia and the links have been provided in the jupyter notebook for the session. This helped us to set out our goals for the topic and explain the performance of algorithms as the complexity of real-world sentences increases. Our main goal was to enable the students to easily expand the datasets themselves and see the change in performance. This is rarely seen in datasets like the STS benchmark (Cer et al., 2017). We believe this is critical to help students reflect on the effect of different data, learning the value of understanding the characteristics of their datasets and appreciate their impact on the performance of algorithms they use to achieve task specific goals. This approach also allowed us to increase the students' curiosity and encourage them to try things out with far more complex use cases, for example the possibility of automatically adding nodes based on these concepts to a knowledge graph.

We started with a simple set of sentences (***Sentence Set 1***) and demonstrating the cosine similarities between sentence vectors obtained by just averaging the individual normalized word vectors.

S1: *Paris is the capital of France*

S2: *Berlin is the capital of Germany*

S3: *French is a Romance language of the Indo-European family*

S4: *German is an Indo-European language which*

belongs to the West Germanic group of Germanic languages

The last two sentences are taken from Wikipedia[1].

It is important to be able to visualize the results during the experimentation. We tried to provide code to the students to be able to easily visualize the results for the examples. We found that using the visualization also made it easy to demonstrate the progressive improvements in the achieved results to the students as the methods were changed.

Figure 1 showed the students that the result is not very impressive.

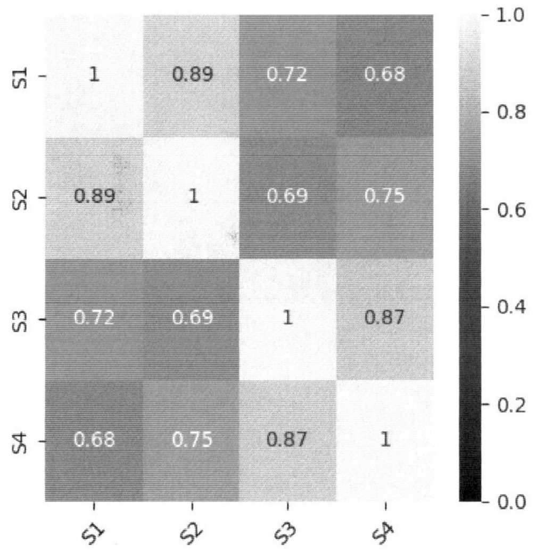

Figure 1: Cosine similarities for ***Sentence Set 1***.

We then suggested a trivial method, that is just using the 'important' words. We thus modified the sentences (***Sentence Set 2***) and demonstrated the improvement brought by this method, as shown in Figure 2.

S1: *Paris capital France*

S2: *Berlin capital Germany*

S3: *French language*

S4: *German language*

Between one step and the other, we activated the students by encouraging them to brainstorm and suggest what a possible next step could be, and we could notice that students were impressed at seeing

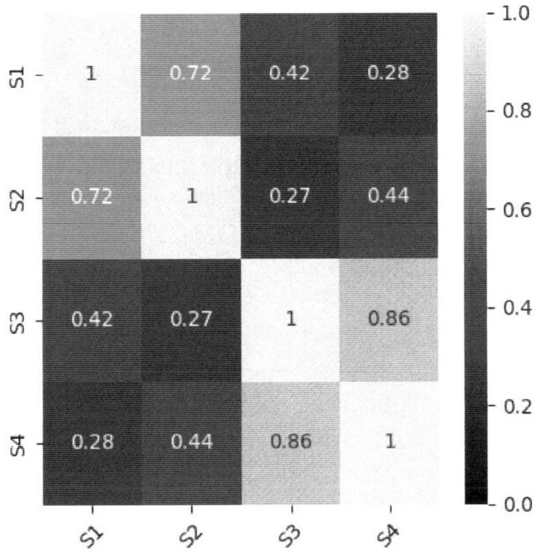

Figure 2: Cosine similarities for ***Sentence Set 2***.

the results of what they had already learnt in the previous units of the course. This also helped in pointing to additional reading material mentioned in the code to understand what could be done to find 'important words' in this context. The heat maps with overlayed similarity scores made it easy to showcase the improved performance.

Then we tried to explain the challenges posed by real-word data by using more complex and longer sentences (***Sentence Set 3***) taken again from the Wikipedia pages related to similar topics[2].

S1: *France has a developed high-income mixed economy characterised by sizeable government involvement economic diversity a skilled labour force and high innovation. For roughly two centuries the French economy has consistently ranked among the ten largest globally.*

S2: *Germany is a federal, parliamentary, representative democratic republic. Federal legislative power is vested in the parliament consisting of the Bundestag (Federal Diet) and Bundesrat (Federal Council), which together form the legislative body.*

S3: *With a population of 80.2 million according to the 2011 German Census, rising to 83.7 million as of 2022, Germany is the most populous*

[1] `https://en.wikipedia.org/wiki/French_language`, `https://en.wikipedia.org/wiki/German_language`

[2] `https://en.wikipedia.org/wiki/France`, `https://en.wikipedia.org/wiki/Germany`. We intentionally chose and mentioned these sources to enable students to later pick their own 'real world' sentences instead of trivialized examples.

country in the European Union, the second-most populous country in Europe after Russia, and the nineteenth-most populous country in the world.

S4: *Each region of France has traditional specialties: cassoulet in the Southwest, choucroute in Alsace, quiche in the Lorraine region, beef bourguignon in Burgundy, provençal tapenade, etc.*

We trivially removed a set of stop words from these sentences (as in the script provided) and showed the results of our trivial method to generate sentence level embeddings and calculate cosine similarity. The students could see that the results as shown in Figure 3 were not what they expected, and they could experiment by replacing the sentences in the code.

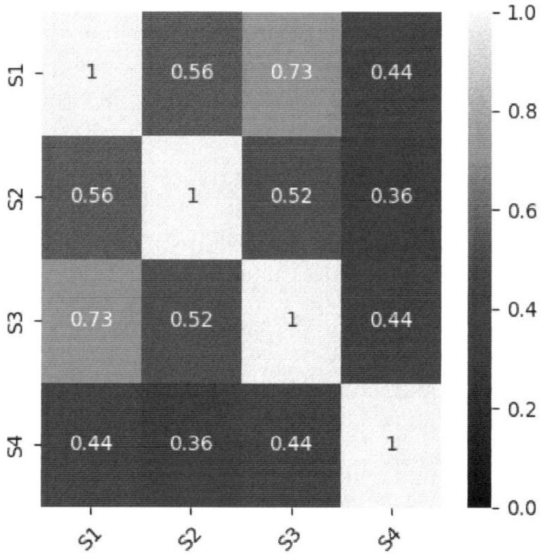

Figure 3: Cosine similarities for ***Sentence Set 3***.

In this way we were able to set up the stage for methods that are built on top of models like BERT (Devlin et al., 2019), to pique the students' interest for the next topics in the course and to show why those methods have high practical significance for many NLP applications. We did not go into the details of the methods, as they will be introduced in later units. Instead, we continued with increasing the complexity of our example sentences and demonstrating the effectiveness of the methods. We expected to create appreciation for the need for methods like attention (Bahdanau et al., 2014) and transformers (Vaswani et al., 2017) that would follow later in the course while still focusing on our chosen topic about sentence embeddings and Semantic Textual Similarity.

We modified the sentence set to have higher diversity in topics and create more complexity for the task by having sentences of very different lengths (***Sentence Set 4***). We believe it is important for students to understand factors such as length and complexity when dealing with real-world data.

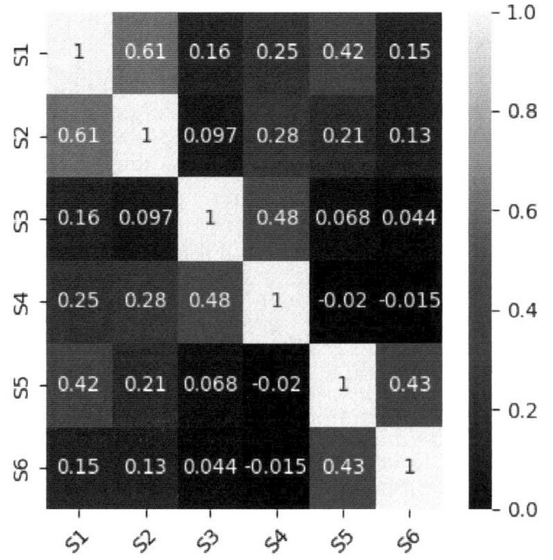

Figure 4: Cosine similarities for ***Sentence Set 4***.

S1: *France has a developed high-income mixed economy characterised by sizeable government involvement economic diversity a skilled labour force and high innovation. For roughly two centuries the French economy has consistently ranked among the ten largest globally.*

S2: *French economy is the world's seventh-largest economy by nominal GDP*

S3: *Germany is a federal, parliamentary, representative democratic republic. Federal legislative power is vested in the parliament consisting of the Bundestag (Federal Diet) and Bundesrat (Federal Council), which together form the legislative body.*

S4: *With a population of 80.2 million according to the 2011 German Census, rising to 83.7 million as of 2022, Germany is the most populous country in the European Union, the second-most populous country in Europe after Russia, and the nineteenth-most populous country in the world.*

S5: *Each region of France has traditional specialties: cassoulet in the Southwest, choucroute* *in Alsace, quiche in the Lorraine region, beef bourguignon in Burgundy, provençal tapenade, etc.*

S6: *A typical French Christmas dish is turkey with chestnuts.*

Another aspect that cannot be neglected in an introductory course with participants from varied disciplines is the computational requirements. The code explicitly mentions the computational needs and how students could use different models based on the computational resources available to them. We used the Sentence Transformers library (`https://www.sbert.net/`) that is based on the methods presented in Reimers and Gurevych (2019) and selected a model that could be easily used on a standard laptop by all students. We additionally mentioned the other models that could be experimented with when more RAM and computational power was available to the students. The result in Figure 4 showed the students how such models could leverage attention mechanism to generate better sentence embeddings.

We ended our demonstration by providing the students with a method to generate data for model finetuning for a task, in order to further separate concepts like economy and cuisine and hinted at possible experiments, for example changing the finetuning dataset source and size and see the effects. The default model we selected in the sample code is important here because students would not be able to run the finetuning on standard laptops for larger models. Completing this task would prepare students for complex real-world applications like domain adaptation of the models for use in semantic information retrieval systems.

At the end we suggested the students to think about collecting the sentences in this form and automatically trying to add them to a graph with a hierarchy of conceptual nodes. To increase their curiosity and willingness to experiment, we provided a hint that this task could provide them a simple basis for more complex representations like Knowledge Graphs, as used for example by Google.

5 Instruction Language

We experimented with a combined usage of German and English. Since the course is taught in German, the slides were created in German and the teaching was also done in German. However, the code comments and additional reading mentioned in the code was in English. The need and intention behind this are twofold. First, most additional reading material related to the topic is available only in English and the documentation for the used libraries is also available only in English. Second, this opens the possibility for students to experiment themselves with creating sample data in German and experiment with multilingual models. Since the text examples are from Wikipedia, getting the data in German and extending it is relatively simple. Interestingly, in the anonymized feedback collected later, the majority of students mentioned that even though they appreciated that the slides and teaching was done in German, they did not consider it necessary. No respondent gave the feedback that having the code comments and additional reading material in English was of any concern to them.

6 Student feedback and possible takeaways

We asked the students to provide anonymized feedback for a set of questions/statements. Eleven students provided the feedback about the session. Figure 5 shows the responses to a subset of questions (translated to English) where students had to select one answer from the four available choices.

Twenty students participated in a more general evaluation of the whole introductory course and were also free to leave comments about the course. Three of them explicitly mentioned the guest lecture on semantic textual similarity as a positive aspect or expressed the wish to see more presentations from the applied domain. Even though the sample size for the results is not large and it is based on a single topic and session, there are some important takeaways for us from this. As most students managed to understand the topic and experimented with the code, we believe that it is feasible to introduce such topics in an introductory course. They also found the availability of code useful. The feedback that most students found the topic relevant for usage in their later careers and that the session increased their interest in the domain, points to the benefits of such an approach.

6.1 Further possibilities and challenges

We realized that one of the shortcomings of our current approach was that we could not evaluate how many students put in the effort to modify or extend the datasets or use different models to conduct their own experiments. We would like to explore how

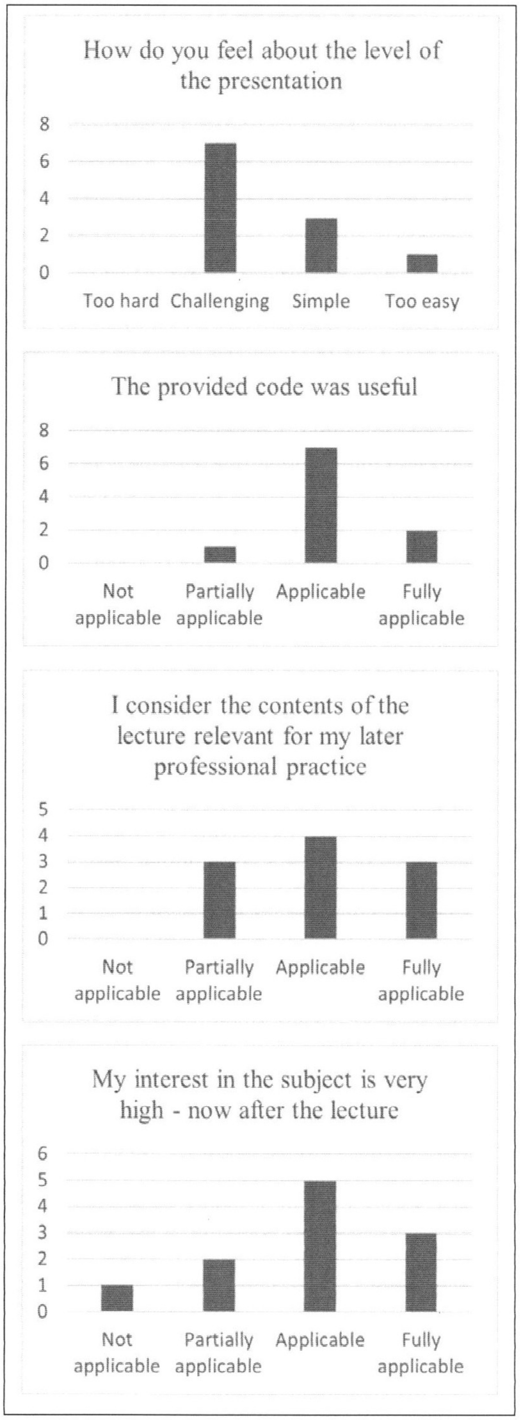

Figure 5: Feedback from the students about the session

we could do this in an introductory course – possibly using an e-learning platform such as Moodle[3] – and how could the students be rewarded for their effort. We believe that the selection of topics is important and not every contemporary topic can be introduced with equal ease in an introductory course.

We also attempted another such session on Instruction Finetuning for LLMs, with a similar goal to offer a demo within the existing constraints on computational power and data. The code and slides for the second unit are available in the GitHub repository at: `https://github.com/saurabhkumar/instruction_tuned_llm`. Additional complexities arise from the computational requirements of the most recent technologies – at least while the Technische Hochschule is in the process of acquiring GPU servers. Until then, we are faced with the challenge of introducing computationally-intensive topics while enabling all students to be able to use the code.

Acknowledgements

We would like to thank the University of Applied Sciences (Technische Hochschule) in Augsburg for providing us this opportunity. We would also like to thank Mr. Klaus Spindler at FORVIA Clean Mobility for the encouragement to conduct the session and in general engagement with students at the University of Applied Sciences (Technische Hochschule) in Augsburg. We are also extremely thankful to all the students who provided their valuable feedback.

References

Eneko Agirre, Daniel Cer, Mona Diab, and Aitor Gonzalez-Agirre. 2012. SemEval-2012 task 6: A pilot on semantic textual similarity. In **SEM 2012: The First Joint Conference on Lexical and Computational Semantics – Volume 1: Proceedings of the main conference and the shared task, and Volume 2: Proceedings of the Sixth International Workshop on Semantic Evaluation (SemEval 2012)*, pages 385–393, Montréal, Canada. Association for Computational Linguistics.

Dzmitry Bahdanau, Kyunghyun Cho, and Yoshua Bengio. 2014. Neural machine translation by jointly learning to align and translate. *arXiv preprint arXiv:1409.0473*.

Daniel Cer, Mona Diab, Eneko Agirre, Iñigo Lopez-Gazpio, and Lucia Specia. 2017. SemEval-2017 task 1: Semantic textual similarity multilingual and crosslingual focused evaluation. In *Proceedings of the 11th International Workshop on Semantic Evaluation (SemEval-2017)*, pages 1–14, Vancouver, Canada. Association for Computational Linguistics.

[3] `https://moodle.org/`

Jacob Devlin, Ming-Wei Chang, Kenton Lee, and Kristina Toutanova. 2019. BERT: Pre-training of deep bidirectional transformers for language understanding. In *Proceedings of the 2019 Conference of the North American Chapter of the Association for Computational Linguistics: Human Language Technologies, Volume 1 (Long and Short Papers)*, pages 4171–4186, Minneapolis, Minnesota. Association for Computational Linguistics.

J. Johnson, M. Douze, and H. Jegou. 2021. Billion-Scale Similarity Search with GPUs. *IEEE Transactions on Big Data*, 7(03):535–547.

Dan Jurafsky and James H Martin. 2023. *Speech and Language Processing*. Jan 7, 2023 draft, accessed here https://web.stanford.edu/ jurafsky/slp3/.

OpenAI. 2023. Gpt-4 technical report.

Nils Reimers and Iryna Gurevych. 2019. Sentence-BERT: Sentence embeddings using Siamese BERT-networks. In *Proceedings of the 2019 Conference on Empirical Methods in Natural Language Processing and the 9th International Joint Conference on Natural Language Processing (EMNLP-IJCNLP)*, pages 3982–3992, Hong Kong, China. Association for Computational Linguistics.

Stephen Robertson and Hugo Zaragoza. 2009. The probabilistic relevance framework: Bm25 and beyond. *Foundations and Trends® in Information Retrieval*, 3(4):333–389.

Romal Thoppilan, Daniel De Freitas, Jamie Hall, Noam Shazeer, Apoorv Kulshreshtha, Heng-Tze Cheng, Alicia Jin, Taylor Bos, Leslie Baker, Yu Du, YaGuang Li, Hongrae Lee, Huaixiu Steven Zheng, Amin Ghafouri, Marcelo Menegali, Yanping Huang, Maxim Krikun, Dmitry Lepikhin, James Qin, Dehao Chen, Yuanzhong Xu, Zhifeng Chen, Adam Roberts, Maarten Bosma, Vincent Zhao, Yanqi Zhou, Chung-Ching Chang, Igor Krivokon, Will Rusch, Marc Pickett, Pranesh Srinivasan, Laichee Man, Kathleen Meier-Hellstern, Meredith Ringel Morris, Tulsee Doshi, Renelito Delos Santos, Toju Duke, Johnny Soraker, Ben Zevenbergen, Vinodkumar Prabhakaran, Mark Diaz, Ben Hutchinson, Kristen Olson, Alejandra Molina, Erin Hoffman-John, Josh Lee, Lora Aroyo, Ravi Rajakumar, Alena Butryna, Matthew Lamm, Viktoriya Kuzmina, Joe Fenton, Aaron Cohen, Rachel Bernstein, Ray Kurzweil, Blaise Aguera-Arcas, Claire Cui, Marian Croak, Ed Chi, and Quoc Le. 2022. Lamda: Language models for dialog applications.

Ashish Vaswani, Noam Shazeer, Niki Parmar, Jakob Uszkoreit, Llion Jones, Aidan N Gomez, Łukasz Kaiser, and Illia Polosukhin. 2017. Attention is all you need. *Advances in neural information processing systems*, 30.

Democratizing Machine Learning for Interdisciplinary Scholars: Reflections on the NLP+CSS Tutorial Series

Katherine Keith*
Williams College
kak5@williams.edu

Ian Stewart*
Pacific Northwest National Laboratory
ian.stewart@pnnl.gov

Abstract

Many scientific fields—including biology, health, education, and the social sciences—use machine learning (ML) to analyze data at an unprecedented scale. However, ML researchers who develop advanced methods rarely provide tutorials showing how to apply these methods. We attempt to democratize the use of ML methods by making them accessible to a broader set of reserachers and practitioners. To that end, we organized a year-long, free, online tutorial series targeted at teaching advanced natural language processing (NLP) methods to computational social science (CSS) scholars. Two organizers worked with fifteen subject matter experts to develop tutorials with hands-on Python code for a range of methods and use cases, from data pre-processing to analyzing temporal language changes. Although live participation was more limited than expected, surveys of participants showed an increase in their perceived knowledge by almost one point on a 7-point Likert scale. Furthermore, participants asked thoughtful questions during tutorials and engaged readily with the content afterwards, as demonstrated by approximately 30K total views of posted tutorial recordings. We distill five principles for democratizing other ML+X tutorials, and we hope that future organizers continue to lower barriers to developing ML skills for researchers of all fields.[1]

1 Introduction

Interest in incorporating machine learning into scientific analyses has exploded in the last two decades. Machine learning (ML)—the process of teaching a machine to predict statistical patterns in data (10)—has gained prominence in biology (9), physics (11), health care (2), and the social sciences (14) inter alia, yielding many successful

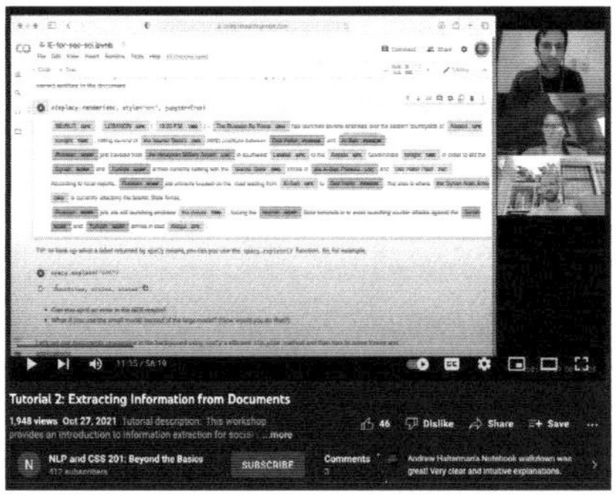

Figure 1: Screen shot of recording for *Tutorial 2: Extracting Information from Documents*. As of May 28 2023, this video had 19K views on YouTube.

"ML+X" collaborations. While this potential impact of ML+X is enormous, many researchers unfamiliar with ML methods face barriers to entry, partly because implementing complex methods can be challenging for those without strong mathematical or programming backgrounds (5). Despite the successes of interdisciplinary work such as computational biology, the learning resources for these research areas are often sparse and not well documented, outside of introductory-level material.

Basic ML methods provide a useful starting place, but applied researchers often have more complex problems. For instance, many social scientists want to use ML to develop deep semantic representations of language or to estimate causal effects. Scholars who seek to advance their understanding of ML beyond the basics are often left searching for tutorial-like materials on their own, a difficult and often time-consuming task. On the other hand, well-meaning ML experts may try to share their expertise through media such as blog posts, but they run the risk of "parachuting" into unfamiliar fields with ill-adapted solutions (1; 19). Finally, many formal avenues for sharing knowledge about ML—such as academic conferences—can systematically *exclude* researchers outside of ML via high fees to

*Both authors contributed equally to this work.
[1]NLP+CSS Tutorial Website: https://nlp-css-201-tutorials.github.io/nlp-css-201-tutorials/

Proceedings of the 1st Workshop on Teaching for NLP, pages 8–18
September 18, 2023. ©2023 Association for Computational Linguistics

access materials.[2]

We take the position that ML researchers can make their methods more accessible and inclusive to researchers outside the field by creating online instruction explicitly tailored to the fields of subject matter experts. Using the NLP+CSS tutorial series we organized in 2021-2022 as a case study, we argue that these interdisciplinary training sessions should incorporate the following **Principles for Democratizing ML+X Tutorials**:

- **P.1** Teach machine learning (ML) methods that are relevant and targeted to specific non-ML fields—e.g. biology, health, or the social sciences
- **P.2** Teach ML methods that are recent and cutting-edge
- **P.3** Lower start-up costs of programming languages and tooling
- **P.4** Provide open-source code that is clearly written, in context, and easily adapted to new problems
- **P.5** Reduce both monetary and time costs for participants

ML+Social Sciences Starting in summer 2021, we put our principles into action and created the *NLP+CSS 201 Online Tutorial Series*. We focused on an applied branch of machine learning to language data—a field called natural language processing (NLP)—aimed at early career researchers in the social sciences. This report reflects on our experience and provides clear takeaways so that others can generalize our NLP + social sciences tutorials to tutorials targeted at other ML+X disciplines.

As we describe in Section 3, we incorporated the principles above into our tutorial series by: (**P.1&P.2**) inviting experts in computational social science (CSS) to each lead a tutorial on a cutting edge NLP method; (**P.3&P.4**) working with the experts to create a learning experience that is hosted in a self-contained interactive development environment in Python—Google CoLaboratory—and uses real-world social science datasets to provide context for the method; and (**P.5**) hosting our tutorials live via Zoom and posting the recordings on YouTube, while providing all the materials and participation without any monetary costs to participants.

2 Related work

2.1 Interdisciplinary tutorials

Researchers specializing in NLP methods have proposed a variety of interdisciplinary tutorials to address social science questions, which we surveyed before we began planning our tutorial series. However, none satisfied all the principles we listed in Section 1. The tutorials presented at the conferences for the Association for Computational Linguistics (ACL)[3]—one of the premiere venues for NLP research—are on the cutting edge of research (+**P.2**) and often include code (+**P.4**), but the ACL tutorials are also often are geared towards NLP researchers rather than researchers in fields outside of computer science (−**P.1**), contain code that assumes substantial background knowledge (−**P.3**) and cost hundreds of dollars to attend (−**P.5**). Other interdisciplinary conferences such as the International Conference on Computational Social Science (IC2S2)[4] also have tutorials that explain recent NLP methods to computational social scientists (+**P.1**,**P.2**,**P.4**), but often the tutorials are presented with inconsistent formats (−**P.3**) and have high attendance costs (−**P.5**). The Summer Institutes in Computational Social Science (SICSS) (18) provide free (+**P.5**) tutorials on NLP methods for social scientists (+**P.1**) with accompanying code (+**P.3&P.4**), but they cover only the basic NLP techniques and not cutting edge methods (−**P.2**), while also limiting their target audience to people already involved with CSS research.[5]

2.2 Online learning

While not without flaws, online learning experiences such as Massive Online Open Courses (MOOCs) have proven useful in higher education when meeting physically is impossible or impractical to due to students' geographic distance (6; 8; 13). Online courses have disrupted traditional education such as in-person college

[2]Among other issues, social science research receives less funding compared to computer science. In 2021, the NSF dispersed $283 million in funding for social sciences, versus $1 billion for computer sciences (from `https://www.nsf.gov/about/congress/118/highlights/cu21.jsp`, accessed 10 August 2022). This lack of funding can prevent social science researchers from attending ML conferences where new tutorials are presented.

[3]`https://www.aclweb.org/portal/acl_sponsored_events`

[4]`https://iscss.org/ic2s2/conference/`

[5]NLP methods include word counting and basic topic modeling: `https://sicss.io/curriculum` (accessed 11 August 2022).

No.	Tutorial Title	Views
	Fall 2021	
T1	Comparing Word Embedding Models	2732
T2	Extracting Information from Documents	19061
T3	Controlling for Text in Causal Inference with Double Machine Learning	676
T4	Text Analysis with Contextualized Topic Models	1043
T5	BERT for Computational Social Scientists	1402
	Spring 2022	
T6	Moving from Words to Phrases when Doing NLP	864
T7	Analyzing Conversations in Python Using ConvoKit	1093
T8	Preprocessing Social Media Text	1269
T9	Aggregated Classification Pipelines	211
T10	Estimating Causal Effects of Aspects of Language with Noisy Proxies	393
T11	Processing Code-mixed Text	693
T12	Word Embeddings for Descriptive Corpus Analysis	413

Table 1: Tutorial content. Order, title, and number of views of the corresponding recordings on YouTube as of May 28 2023. Full abstracts of each tutorial are provided in the appendix, Table 3.

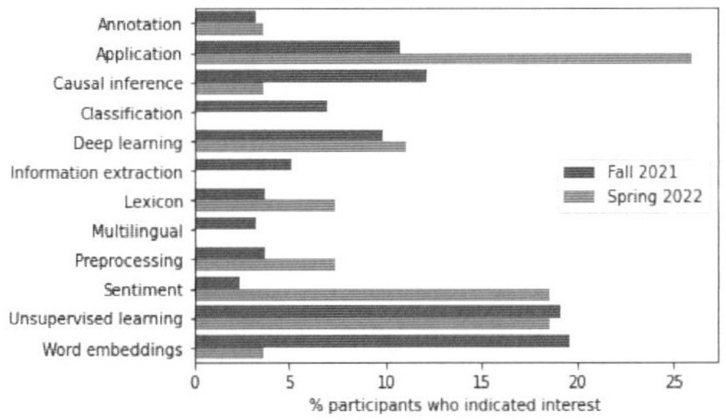

Figure 2: Distribution of interest in NLP methods indicated in initial interest surveys.

classes (22), but they may eventually prove most useful as a supplement rather than a replacement to traditional education (21). For one, computer science students have found online learning useful when it incorporates interactive components such as hands-on exercises which may not be possible to execute during a lecture (15; 20). Additionally, while the centralized approach to traditional education can provide useful structure for students new to a domain, the decentralized approach of many online courses can provide room for socialization and creativity in content delivery (23; 24). We intended our tutorial series to fit into the developing paradigm of online education as a decentralized and interactive experience, which would not replace but supplement social science education in machine learning. However, our tutorial series differs from MOOCs in that we limit the time committment for each topic to one hour (+**P.5**) and each tutorial hour is meant to be stand-alone so that researchers can watch only the topics that are relevant to them.

3 Methods for Tutorial Series: Process and Timeline

We describe our process and timeline for creating the tutorial series with the hope that future ML+X tutorial series organizers can copy or build from our experience. Throughout our planning process, we based our decisions on the five principles mentioned earlier (**P.1-P.5**). Our tutorial series spanned two semesters: Fall 2021 (August through December) and Spring 2022 (February through May). The tutorial content is summarized in Table 1.

3.1 Interest survey

To select relevant methods for the tutorial series (**P.1**), we distributed a survey via our personal Twitter accounts, via a Google group mailing list that we created at the beginning of the fall 2021 semester, and via topically related mailing lists (e.g. a political methods list-serv). We asked participants to list the methods that they would be most interested in learning about during a tutorial, which we then grouped into categories based on underlying similarities.

The distribution of interest categories is shown in Figure 2. As expected, the responses covered many different NLP applications (17), including data preparation (preprocessing, multilingual), conversion of text to relevant constructs (information extraction, word embeddings, deep learning), and downstream analysis (causal inference, application). Most participants expressed interest in word embeddings, unsupervised learning, and downstream applications of NLP methods, which aligns with the current popularity of such methods.

Lessons learned Since we typically publish in NLP venues, we took a prescriptive approach to choosing the tutorial methods to present, in an attempt to more actively shape the field of computational social science (addressing **P.1**& **P.2**). We used the results of the survey to brainstorm potential topics for each upcoming semester, but did not restrict ourselves to only the most popular methods. While useful, the interest surveys revealed a disconnect between our ideal tutorials, which focused on advanced NLP methods, and the participants' ideal tutorials, e.g. entry-level methods with immediate downstream results. For example, many participants in the Spring 2022 interest survey mentioned sentiment analysis, a well-studied area of NLP (3) that we considered to be more introductory-level and sometimes unreliable (7). This was one source of tension between our expectations and those of the participants, and future tutorial series organizers may want to focus their efforts on highly-requested topics to ensure consistent participation and satisfaction (**P.1**).

3.2 Leader recruitment

Aligning with **P.2**, we recruited other NLP experts who worked on cutting-edge methods to lead each individual tutorial.[6] To ensure **P.3**, we also met with the tutorial hosts to agree on a common format for the programming platform—Google CoLaboratory with Python[7]—and to help them understand the tutorials' objectives. The process involved several meetings: an introduction meeting to scope the tutorial, and at least one planning meeting to review the slides and code to be presented. Normally, this process was guided by a paper or project for which the tutorial leader had code available. For example, the leader of tutorial T4 was able to leverage an extensive code base already tested by her lab.

Lessons learned During the planning process, we were forced to plan the tutorials one at a time due to complicated schedules among the leaders. We spread out the planning meetings during the semester so that the planning meetings would begin roughly two to three weeks before the associated tutorial. We strongly encouraged leaders to provide their code to us at least one week in advance to give us time to review it, but we found this difficult to enforce due to time constraints on the leaders' side (e.g. some leaders had to prioritize other teaching commitments). Future organizers should set up a consistent schedule for contacting leaders in advance and agree with leaders on tutorial code that is relatively new and usable (**P.2**& **P.4**) without presenting an undue burden for the leader, e.g. re-using existing code bases.

[6]We recruited tutorial leaders through our own social networks and through mutual acquaintances. We targeted post-doctoral fellows, early-career professors, and advanced graduate students.

[7]`https://colab.research.google.com/`

3.3 Participant recruitment

Even if we guaranteed **P.1**-**P.5** with the content developed, recruiting social science participants was essential to the success of our tutorial series. In September 2021, we set up an official mailing list through Google Groups and advertised it on social media and other methods-related list-servs.[8] The mailing list eventually hosted 396 unique participants. For all tutorials, we set up a RSVP system using Google Forms for participants to sign up, and we provided an RSVP link up to one week before each tutorial. We chose this "walled garden" approach to discourage anti-social activity such as Zoom-bombing which is often made easier by open invitation links (12), and to provide tutorial leaders with a better sense of their participants.

Lesson learned This process revealed significant drop-out: between 10-30% of people who signed up actually attended the tutorial. While the reasons for the drop-out remained unclear, participants may have signed up for the tutorial as a back-up to an existing obligation, under the assumption that the tutorial recording would be available later. Although asynchronous learning can be effective in some cases, the low number of live participants was somewhat discouraging to the tutorial hosts.

3.4 Running the tutorials

During the tutorials, we wanted to ensure low start-up cost of the programming environment (**P.3**) and well-written code that participants could use immediately after the tutorials (**P.4**). We designed each tutorial to run for slightly under 60 minutes, to account for time required for introductions, transitions, and follow-up questions. The tutorial leader began the session with a presentation to explain the method of interest with minimal math, using worked examples on toy data and examples of prior research that leveraged the method.

After 20-30 minutes of presentation, the tutorial leader switched to showing the code written in a Google CoLaboratory Python notebook (**P.3**), which allows users to run modular blocks of code. The leader would load or generate a simple text dataset, often no more than several hundred documents in size, to illustrate the method's application. Depending on the complexity of the method, the

[8]The Google Group was only accessible to participants with Google Mail accounts, which in retrospect likely discouraged some participants who only use institutional email accounts.

▾ What is a Neural Topic model?

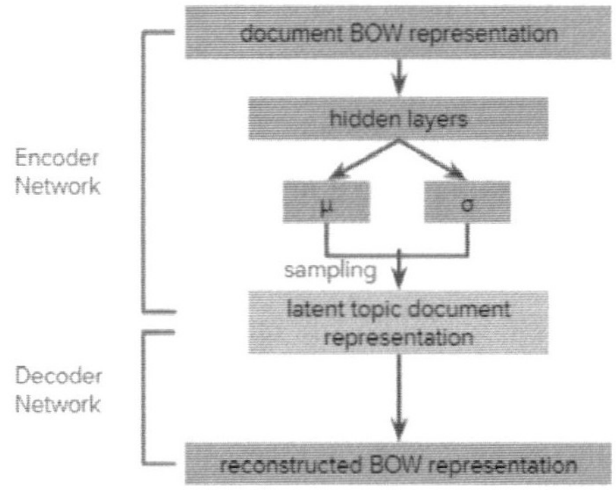

(a)

{"id": 2, "text": "Do you think it is fundamentally right that the state should financially support the provision of childcare for working parents (through tax allowances or subsidies)?", "topic": "Welfare"}
{"id": 4, "text": "Should a 24-week period of \"parental leave\" be introduced in addition to the existing maternity insurance benefits?", "topic": "Welfare"}
{"id": 6, "text": "The disability insurance system no longer provides for disability benefits to be paid for pain disorders that cannot be objectively proved (e.g. as a result of whiplash injury). Do you approve?", "topic": "Welfare"}
{"id": 7, "text": "Would you support a national hospital planning scheme even if it might lead to the closure of hospitals?", "topic": "Healthcare"}
{"id": 9, "text": "Do you think it's right that certain forms of alternative medicine are once again to be reimbursed under the basic healthcare system?", "topic": "Healthcare"}

(b)

```
[ ] ctm.get_topic_lists(5)

[['expanded', 'framework', 'tax', 'taxation', 'uber'],
 ['petrol', 'switzerland', 'co', 'fossil', 'fuels'],
 ['chf', 'minimum', 'wage', 'full', 'listed'],
 ['government', 'mountain', 'sites', 'focused', 'public'],
 ['refugees', 'united', 'accept', 'unhcr', 'asylum'],
 ['contributions', 'weak', 'cantons', 'road', 'women'],
 ['well', 'consumption', 'possession', 'legalize', 'soft'],
 ['schools', 'subjects', 'pe', 'swimming', 'events'],
 ['openly', 'telephone', 'security', 'political', 'socialization'],
 ['eu', 'trade', 'post', 'reliefs', 'agreement'],
 ['support', 'federal', 'government', 'financial', 'equal'],
 ['companies', 'human', 'relaxed', 'compliance', 'environmental']]
```

(c)

Figure 3: Excerpts from the tutorial on topic modeling (T4), demonstrating (a) the application of a neural model to (b) text from politicians' interviews, which produces (c) word lists for inductively discovered topics.

leader might start with some basic steps and then show the students increasingly complicated code snippets. In general, the leaders walked the students through separate modules that showed different aspects of the method in question. During the topic modeling session (T4), the leader showed first how to train the topic model, then provided extensive examples of what the topic output looked like and how it should be interpreted (e.g. top words per topic, example documents with high topic probabilities).[9] As a point of comparison, the leader also would often show the output of a simpler "baseline" model to demonstrate the superior performance of the tutorial's more advanced method. We show excerpts from the tutorial notebook on topic modeling in Figure 3, which includes an overview of the topic model, a sample of the text data which relates to politics, and the resulting learned "topics" as lists of words.

[9]Topic models are used to identify latent groupings for words in a document, e.g. a health-related topic might include "exercise" and "nutrition." (4)

Lessons learned To encourage critical thinking, some of the tutorial leaders provided questions or exercises in the Colab notebooks for students to complete at a later time. The leader of the information extraction tutorial (T2) created an exercise for students to parse sentences from news text related to military activity, and then to extract all sentences that described an attack between armies. Some of these exercises posed challenges to participants who lacked experience with the data structures or function calls involved in the code. For future tutorials, leaders should consider simply showing participants how to solve a simple exercise (e.g. live-coding) rather than expecting participants to attack the problem on their own.

3.5 Participation during tutorials

During each tutorial, we—the organizers—acted as facilitators to help the leaders handle questions and manage time effectively. The leaders were often unable to see the live chat while presenting, and we therefore found natural break points in the presentation to answer questions sent to the chat. While we allowed for written and spoken questions, participants preferred to ask questions in the chat, possibly to avoid interrupting the presenter and to allow them to answer asynchronously.

Participants were encouraged to test out the code on their own during the tutorial, and the code was generally written to execute quickly without significant lag for e.g. downloads or model training (**P.3**). This often required the leaders to run some of the code in advance to automate less interesting components of the tutorial, e.g. selecting the optimal number of topics for the topic model.

Lessons learned Based on some of the questions received, participants seemed to engage well with the code and to follow up with some of the methods. Participants asked between 1 and 15 questions per tutorial (median 5). We show example questions from the tutorials with the largest number of questions in Table 2. The questions cover both simple closed-answer questions ("Can the code provide

Tutorial	Question sample
T1	Is there a reason that we're using word2vec rather than other models such as fastText? What does Euclidean distance between embeddings mean? Does word2vec work on short "documents" such as Twitter data?
T4	How is the bag of words representation combined with contextualized representation? How should someone choose the model to use for this component? What models does your package support?
T6	Are Phrases mostly Nouns since Nouns are the ones that have multi-words? Have you tried this model in languages other than English? How was the PhraseBert model trained?
T7	How do you keep track of who's responding to what previous utterance? How do you create a conversation corpus from scratch? Can the code provide statistics or summary for each speaker or utterance?
T9	Could you interpret a well-calibrated model as estimating the moral outrage in a post? Do choices in favor of hard modeling an aggregation techniques lead to higher values in outcome measurement? What would you recommend to handle annotator disagreement when the task is to label spans inside the text?

Table 2: Example questions from tutorial sessions. Some wording changed for clarity.

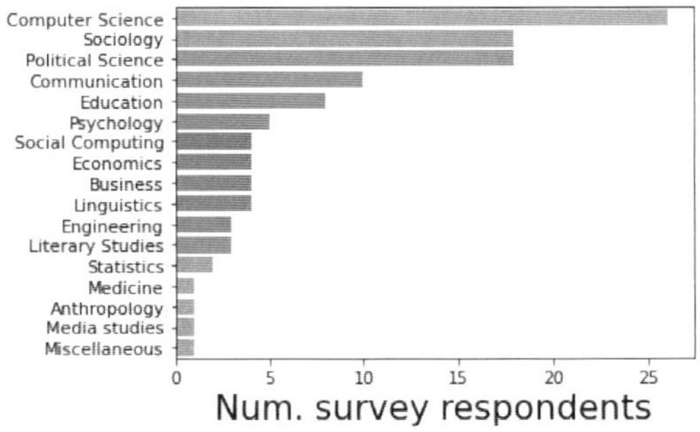

(a)

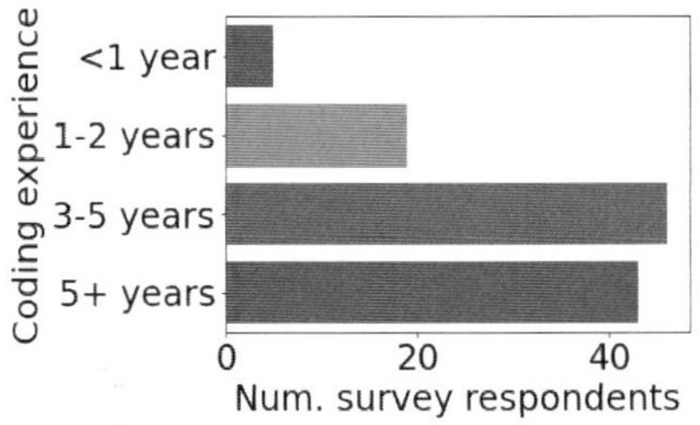

(b)

	μ	σ
Pre-Q1–Learned from code (1-5)	4.00	0.94
Pre-Q2–Learned from content (1-5)	4.24	0.90
Pre- vs post-survey	E[**Post-Q3**] - E[**Pre-Q3**]	
Knowledge about the topic (1-7)	0.77*	

(c)

Figure 4: Participant responses for the survey sent during the live tutorials (aggregated from T4-T12). Figure (a) indicates participant disciplines **(Pre-Q1)** and (b) coding experience **(Pre-Q2)**. Table (c) shows *(top)* the mean (μ) and standard deviation (σ) on a 5-point Likert scale for **Post-Q1&2** and *(bottom)* for the question about participants' self-rated knowledge about the topic graded on a 7-point Likert scale, the expected value of the post survey minus the expected value of the pre-survey (E[**Post-Q3**] - E[**Pre-Q3**]). *Indicates statistical significance with p-value $< 10^{-5}$ via a two-sided T-test.

statistics") and more complicated open-ended questions ("How should someone choose the model to use"). While the number of questions was relatively low overall, the participants who asked questions were engaged and curious about the limitations and ramifications of the methods being presented. To improve participant engagement via questions, future leaders may find it useful to pose their own questions throughout the code notebook ("what do you think would happen if we applied method X while setting parameter Z=1?") as a way to guide the participants' curiosity.

4 Analysis of Effectiveness

4.1 Pre- and post-surveys during live tutorials

During the live portions of the tutorials, we distributed an optional survey to participants at the beginning and end of the one-hour sessions.[10] The pre-survey consisted of three questions in a Google form: **(Pre-Q1)** *Academic discipline background* in which participants chose one of the given disciplines or wrote their own; **(Pre-Q2)** *How many years of experience in coding/data analysis do you have?* which had four options; and **(Pre-Q3)** *How much do you currently know about the topic?* which was judged on a 7-point Likert scale with 1 described as *I know nothing about the topic*, 4 described as *I could possibly use the methods in my research, but I'd need guidance* and 7 described as *Knowledgeable, I could teach this tutorial.* The post-survey consisted of four questions: **(Post-Q1)** *Code: How much did you learn from the hands-on code aspect of the tutorial?*; **(Post-Q2)** *Content: How much did you learn from the content part of the tutorial?*; **(Post-Q3)** *Now, after the tutorial, how much do you currently know about the*

[10]During T1-T3 we were prototyping the series, so we only distributed the surveys for T4-T12.

topic? and **(Post-Q4)** *Any suggestions or changes we should make for the next tutorial?*. Questions 1 and 2 were judged on a 5-point Likert scale with 1 described as *Learned nothing new* and 5 described as *Learned much more than I could have on my own*. Question 3 was judged on the same 7-point Likert scale as the analogous question in the pre-survey.

Results We report aggregated survey responses in Figure 4. Across the eight tutorials for which we collected data, the pre-surveys had 113 respondents total and the post-surveys had 63 respondents. Figure 4a shows the results of the breakdown by academic discipline or background **(Pre-Q1)**. The three largest areas of participation came from the fields of computer science, sociology, and political science. Figure 4b shows that our participants actually had quite a lot of experience in coding or data analysis **(Pre-Q2)**–78.8% of participants who responded had three or greater years of experience in coding.

Analyzing **Post-Q1** about how much they learned from code, participants responded with $\mu = 4, \sigma = 0.94$. **Post-Q2** about learning from content was similar with $\mu = 4.24, \sigma = 0.9$. Interpreting these results, many participants perceived a high degree of learning from attending the live tutorials. We measure the pre- to post-survey learning by computing the difference between the mean of **Post-Q3** and mean of **Pre-Q3**, and we find a difference of 0.77.[11] We ran a two-sided T-test to see if the pre- versus post-survey differences were greater than zero with statistical significance, which produced a t-value of 4.16 and a p-value less than 10^{-5}. While seemingly small in aggregate, this change represents a consistent growth in perceived knowledge among participants that is surprising considering the relatively short tutorial length of one hour. Manually reading the responses from **(Post-Q4)**, participants described very positive experiences, including "very good tutorial" "Excellent tutorial!!!" and "very helpful."

Lessons learned As Figure 4a shows, we were successful in recruiting participants from a wide variety of social science disciplines. However, computer science or data science—top-most bar in Figure 4a—was the most represented field. In reflection, having another organizer who was primarily focused on social science, rather than NLP, would help us recruit more CSS-oriented participants and would align better with **P.1**. Responses from **Post-Q4** also indicated that the tutorials were not long enough for some participants. One participant said "It would be great to make something like this into a multi-part tutorial. It seemed like too much new material for 1 hour." Some suggestions for future tutorial organizers could be to make the tutorials 2-3 hours long. In the first hour, the tutorial could provide an overview, followed by more advanced topics or practice in hours 2-3. It's difficult to satisfy the trade-offs of (1) audience attention bandwidth and (2) fully explaining a particular method. We also could have improved how we set audience expectations: introducing the tutorials as a crash course and explaining that participants should expect to spend 4-5 hours on their own afterwards to learn the material in depth. Furthermore, future leaders may want to require or strongly encourage participation in the surveys to improve data collection as we had relatively low participation rates.[12]

4.2 Downstream impact

Despite the relatively low synchronous participation (roughly 4-30 participants per session), the views on the tutorial videos posted to YouTube showed consistent growth during the tutorial series and even afterward, culminating in approximately 30K total views. In addition, the tutorial materials were showcased on the website for the Summer Institute for Computational Social Science,[13] and several tutorial leaders presented their tutorials again at an international social science conference, having prepared relevant materials as part of our series (**P.4**). [14] The tutorial series may therefore have the greatest impact not for the synchronous participants but instead for the large and growing audience of researchers who discover the materials after the fact and may not have the re-

[11]Ideally, we would look not at the aggregate participant responses but instead test the pairwise differences for each individual's pre- versus post-survey. However, we found that only 18 participants could be matched from pre- to post-survey due to drop-out, which is too small for pairwise significance testing.

[12]After all the tutorials were presented, we also sent a survey to the mailing list to ask about how much participants had learned from the tutorials and whether they used the material in their own work. We received only five responses total, therefore we do not present statistics here.

[13]Accessed 15 October 2022: `https://sicss.io/overview`.

[14]International Conference on Web and Social Media 2022, accessed 15 October 2022: `https://www.icwsm.org/2022/index.html/#tutorials-schedule`

sources to learn about the methods via traditional methods (**P.5**). The success of the tutorials in other contexts also points to the beginning of a virtuous cycle, in which tutorial leaders test-drive their work in an informal setting and then present a more formal version at an academic conference.

5 Conclusion

Future improvements Reflecting on our organization experience, we suggest the following improvements for future ML+X tutorial organizers:

- Despite the results of the pre-tutorial interest surveys, we made curatorial decisions about the content and we cannot be sure that we satisfied the needs of what participants wanted versus what we thought was important. Future organizers may achieve higher participation by focusing on methods with high public interest, regardless of their lower perceived utility by subject area experts.
- The two co-organizers were both computer scientists, and we largely leveraged a computer science professional network for recruitment. Future renditions would ideally include a social scientist co-organizer to provide better insight into current ML needs and desires among researchers (**P.1**), as well as helping tutorial participants feel more at ease with complicated ML methods.
- We found that participants did not consistently engage in the hands-on coding segments of the tutorials. We recommend that future tutorial leaders either simplify the hands-on coding for short sessions, or follow up on the tutorial with additional "office hours" for interested students to try out the code and ask further questions about the method (**P.3**). Similar to some computer science courses, this approach might have a lecture component and a separate "recitation" session for asking questions about the code.
- In the early stages of the tutorial series, we focused more on executing the tutorials rather than collecting quantitative data about the participants' experience. This makes it difficult to judge some aspects of the tutorials' success, especially how the tutorials were received by participants with different backgrounds and expectations. With more extensive evaluation and participation in surveys, we hope that future organizers will make quicker and more effective improvements during the course of a tutorial series.

Successes Despite these drawbacks, we believe our tutorial series succeeded in its goal—to help social scientists advance their skills beyond introductory NLP methods. We hope other ML+X tutorials can build from our successes:

- We accumulated approximately 30K total views among our public recordings. Thus, we'd encourage future ML+X organizers to put even more effort into the recordings rather than live sessions.
- Although participants came in skilled—78.8% of participants who responded had three or greater years of experience in coding (Figure 4b)–they reported aggregate increase in perceived knowledge of the methods presented—0.77 on a 7-point Likert scale.
- We generated education content for a diverse set of relevant and new NLP methods (**P.1**&**P.2**) that can accelerate social science research. The subject matter experts who led the tutorials were able to translate complicated ML concepts into understandable, step-by-step lessons. We hope future ML+X organizers can take inspiration from these tutorials' choice of content and social organization.
- Our tutorials have produced ready-to-use, modular, and freely available Python code with a low barrier to entry (**P.3**,**P.4**,**P.5**), which will provide "scaffolding" to future students seeking to start their own projects (16). We envision future ML+X organizers using this codebase as a template for releasing code in their own domain.

As machine learning methods become more available and more powerful, scientists may feel encouraged to implement these methods within their own domain-specific research. We believe tutorial series such as the one described in this report will help guide these researchers on their journey. Like the tutorials themselves, we hope that our *Principles for Democratizing ML+X Tutorials* (**P.1**–**P.5**) will be used as springboard toward more open and inclusive learning experiences for all researchers. Rather than wait for top-down solutions, we encourage other ML practitioners to get involved and shape the future of applied science by sharing their knowledge directly with scholars eager to know more.

Acknowledgments

We are deeply grateful for financial assistance from a Social Science Research Council (SSRC)/Summer Institutes in Computational Social Science (SICSS) Research Grant. We thank SIGCSE reviewers and various computer science education experts for their feedback on initial drafts. We thank the fourteen additional organizers who generously donated their expertise and time to making these tutorials possible: Connor Gilroy, Sandeep Soni, Andrew Halterman, Emaad Manzoor, Silvia Terragni, Maria Antoniak, Abe Handler, Shufan Wang, Jonathan Chang, Steve Wilson, Dhanya Sridhar, Monojit Choudhury, Sanad Rizvi, and Neha Kennard.

References

[1] ADAME, F. Meaningful collaborations can end "helicopter research". *Nature* (2021).

[2] BEAM, A. L., AND KOHANE, I. S. Big data and machine learning in health care. *Jama 319*, 13 (2018), 1317–1318.

[3] BIRJALI, M., KASRI, M., AND BENI-HSSANE, A. A comprehensive survey on sentiment analysis: Approaches, challenges and trends. *Knowledge-Based Systems 226* (2021), 107134.

[4] BLEI, D. M., NG, A. Y., AND JORDAN, M. I. Latent Dirichlet Allocation. *Journal of machine Learning research 3*, Jan (2003), 993–1022.

[5] CAI, C. J., AND GUO, P. J. Software developers learning machine learning: Motivations, hurdles, and desires. In *2019 IEEE symposium on visual languages and human-centric computing (VL/HCC)* (2019), IEEE, pp. 25–34.

[6] DE WAARD, I., ABAJIAN, S., GALLAGHER, M. S., HOGUE, R., KESKIN, N., KOUTROPOULOS, A., AND RODRIGUEZ, O. C. Using mLearning and MOOCs to understand chaos, emergence, and complexity in education. *The International Review of Research in Open and Distributed Learning 12*, 7 (2011), 94–115.

[7] DÍAZ, M., JOHNSON, I., LAZAR, A., PIPER, A. M., AND GERGLE, D. Addressing age-related bias in sentiment analysis. In *Proceedings of the 2018 chi conference on human factors in computing systems* (2018), pp. 1–14.

[8] HARASIM, L. Shift happens: Online education as a new paradigm in learning. *The Internet and higher education 3*, 1-2 (2000), 41–61.

[9] JONES, D. T. Setting the standards for machine learning in biology. *Nature Reviews Molecular Cell Biology 20*, 11 (2019), 659–660.

[10] JORDAN, M. I., AND MITCHELL, T. M. Machine learning: Trends, perspectives, and prospects. *Science 349*, 6245 (2015), 255–260.

[11] KARNIADAKIS, G. E., KEVREKIDIS, I. G., LU, L., PERDIKARIS, P., WANG, S., AND YANG, L. Physics-informed machine learning. *Nature Reviews Physics 3*, 6 (2021), 422–440.

[12] LING, C., BALCI, U., BLACKBURN, J., AND STRINGHINI, G. A First Look at Zoombombing. In *2021 IEEE Symposium on Security and Privacy (SP)* (2021), IEEE, pp. 1452–1467.

[13] MARCELINO, M. J., PESSOA, T., VIEIRA, C., SALVADOR, T., AND MENDES, A. J. Learning computational thinking and Scratch at distance. *Computers in Human Behavior 80* (2018), 470–477.

[14] MASON, W., VAUGHAN, J. W., AND WALLACH, H. Computational social science and social computing, 2014.

[15] MEERBAUM-SALANT, O., ARMONI, M., AND BEN-ARI, M. Learning computer science concepts with scratch. *Computer Science Education 23*, 3 (2013), 239–264.

[16] NAM, D., KIM, Y., AND LEE, T. The effects of scaffolding-based courseware for the Scratch programming learning on student problem solving skill. In *Proceedings of the 18th International Conference on Computers in Education* (2010), vol. 723, Asia-Pacific Society for Computers in Education Putrajaya, Malaysia, p. 727.

[17] NGUYEN, D., LIAKATA, M., DEDEO, S., EISENSTEIN, J., MIMNO, D., TROMBLE, R., AND WINTERS, J. How we do things with words: Analyzing text as social and cultural data. *Frontiers in Artificial Intelligence 3* (2020), 62.

[18] SHARLACH, M. Summer institute advances social science in the digital age. *Princeton Office of Engineering Communications* (2019).

[19] SUMMERS, R. M. Artificial intelligence of COVID-19 imaging: a hammer in search of a nail. *Radiology* (2021).

[20] TANG, T., RIXNER, S., AND WARREN, J. An environment for learning interactive programming. In *Proceedings of the 45th ACM technical symposium on Computer science education* (2014), pp. 671–676.

[21] TWIGG, C. A. Models for online learning. *Educause review 38* (2003), 28–38.

[22] VARDI, M. Y. Will MOOCs destroy academia? *Communications of the ACM 55*, 11 (2012), 5–5.

[23] WALLACE, A. Social learning platforms and the flipped classroom. In *2013 Second International Conference on E-Learning and E-Technologies in Education (ICEEE)* (2013), IEEE, pp. 198–200.

[24] WILEY, D. A., AND EDWARDS, E. K. Online self-organizing social systems: The decentralized future of online learning. *Quarterly review of distance education 3*, 1 (2002), 33–46.

Appendix

We provide the full abstracts of the tutorials in Table 3, which the tutorial leaders wrote in coordination with the organizers.

	Summary
T1	We'll demonstrate an extension of the use of word embedding models by fitting multiple models on a social science corpus (using gensim's word2vec implementation), then aligning and comparing those models. This method is used to explore group variation and temporal change. We'll discuss some tradeoffs and possible extensions of this approach.
T2	This workshop provides an introduction to information extraction for social science–techniques for identifying specific words, phrases, or pieces of information contained within documents. It focuses on two common techniques, named entity recognition and dependency parses, and shows how they can provide useful descriptive data about the civil war in Syria. The workshop uses the Python library spaCy, but no previous experience is needed beyond familiarity with Python.
T3	Establishing causal relationships is a fundamental goal of scientific research. Text plays an increasingly important role in the study of causal relationships across domains especially for observational (non-experimental) data. Specifically, text can serve as a valuable "control" to eliminate the effects of variables that threaten the validity of the causal inference process. But how does one control for text, an unstructured and nebulous quantity? In this tutorial, we will learn about bias from confounding, motivation for using text as a proxy for confounders, apply a "double machine learning" framework that uses text to remove confounding bias, and compare this framework with non-causal text dimensionality reduction alternatives such as topic modeling.
T4	Most topic models still use Bag-Of-Words (BoW) document representations as input. These representations, though, disregard the syntactic and semantic relationships among the words in a document, the two main linguistic avenues to coherent text. Recently, pre-trained contextualized embeddings have enabled exciting new results in several NLP tasks, mapping a sentence to a vector representation. Contextualized Topic Models (CTM) combine contextualized embeddings with neural topic models to increase the quality of the topics. Moreover, using multilingual embeddings allows the model to learn topics in one language and predict them for documents in unseen languages, thus addressing a task of zero-shot cross-lingual topic modeling.
T5	What is BERT? How do you use it? What kinds of computational social science projects would BERT be most useful for? Join for a conceptual overview of this popular natural language processing (NLP) model as well as a hands-on, code-based tutorial that demonstrates how to train and fine-tune a BERT model using HuggingFace's popular Python library.
T6	Most people starting out with NLP think of text in terms of single-word units called "unigrams." But many concepts in documents can't be represented by single words. For instance, the single words "New" and "York" can't really represent the concept "New York." In this tutorial, you'll get hands-on practice using the phrasemachine package and the Phrase-BERT model to 1) extract multi-word expressions from a corpus of U.S. Supreme Court arguments and 2) use such phrases for downstream analysis tasks, such as analyzing the use of phrases among different groups or describing latent topics from a corpus.
T7	ConvoKit is a Python toolkit for analyzing conversational data. It implements a number of conversational analysis methods and algorithms spanning from classical NLP techniques to the latest cutting edge, and also offers a database of conversational corpora in a standardized format. This tutorial will walk through an example of how to use ConvoKit, starting from loading a conversational corpus and building up to running several analyses and visualizations.
T8	hmm howwww should we think about our #NLProc preprocessing pipeline when it comes to informal TEXT written by social media users?!? In this tutorial, we'll discuss some interesting features of social media text data and how we can think about handling them when doing computational text analyses. We will introduce some Python libraries and code that you can use to process text and give you a chance to experiment with some real data from platforms like Twitter and Reddit.
T9	NLP has helped massively scale-up previously small-scale content analyses. Many social scientists train NLP classifiers and then measure social constructs (e.g sentiment) for millions of unlabeled documents which are then used as variables in downstream causal analyses. However, there are many points when one can make hard (non-probabilistic) or soft (probabilistic) assumptions in pipelines that use text classifiers: (a) adjudicating training labels from multiple annotators, (b) training supervised classifiers, and (c) aggregating individual-level classifications at inference time. In practice, propagating these hard versus soft choices down the pipeline can dramatically change the values of final social measurements. In this tutorial, we will walk through data and Python code of a real-world social science research pipeline that uses NLP classifiers to infer many users' aggregate "moral outrage" expression on Twitter. Along the way, we will quantify the sensitivity of our pipeline to these hard versus soft choices.
T10	Does the politeness of an email or a complaint affect how quickly someone responds to it? This question requires a causal inference: how quickly would someone have responded to an email had it not been polite? With observational data, causal inference requires ruling out all the other reasons why polite emails might be correlated with fast responses. To complicate matters, aspects of language such as politeness are not labeled in observed datasets. Instead, we typically use lexicons or trained classifiers to predict these properties for each text, creating a (probably noisy) proxy of the linguistic aspect of interest. In this talk, I'll first review the challenges of causal inference from observational data. Then, I'll use the motivating example of politeness and response times to highlight the specific challenges to causal inference introduced by working with text and noisy proxies. Next, I'll introduce recent results that establish assumptions and a methodology under which valid causal inference is possible. Finally, I'll demonstrate this methodology: we'll use semi-synthetic data and adapt a text representation method to recover causal effect estimates.
T11	Code-mixing, i.e., the mixing of two or more languages in a single utterance or conversation, is an extremely common phenomenon in multilingual societies. It is amply present in user-generated text, especially in social media. Therefore, CSS research that handles such text requires to process code-mixing; there are also interesting CSS and socio-linguistic questions around the phenomenon of code-mixing itself. In this tutorial, we will equip you with some basic tools and techniques for processing code-mixed text, starting with hands-on experiments with word-level language identification, all the way up to methods for building code-mixed text classifiers using massively multilingual language models.
T12	Word embeddings such as word2vec have recently garnered attention as potentially useful tools for analysis in social science. They promise an unsupervised method to quantify the connotations of words, and compare these across time or different subgroups. However, when training or using word embeddings, researchers may find that they don't work as well as expected, or produce unreplicable results. We focus on three subtle issues in their use that could result in misleading observations: (1) indiscriminate use of analogical reasoning, which has been shown to underperform on many types of analogies; (2) the surprising prevalence of polysemous words and distributional similarity of antonyms, both leading to counterintuitive results; and (3) instability in nearest-neighbor distances caused by sensitivity to noise in the training process. Through demonstrations, we will learn how to detect, understand, and most importantly mitigate the effects of these issues.

Table 3: Tutorial abstracts, provided by leaders.

Working at your own Pace: Computer-based Learning for CL

Anselm Knebusch and **Ulrike Padó**
Hochschule für Technik Stuttgart
Schellingstr. 24
70176 Stuttgart
firstname.lastname@hft-stuttgart.de

Abstract

Introductory Computational Linguistics (CL) classes are often made up of students from different fields of study, most commonly CL, Linguistics or Computer Science (CS) – all of whom have different expertise and perspectives on the subject. Even among students of a single program, learning speeds and previous experience vary widely.

The teaching method of Computer-based Learning (CBL) was developed specifically to address this type of heterogeneity among students. It aims to combine the advantages of on-line and in-presence teaching: Students do self-paced work on video inputs, feedback tests and practical exercises while the professor is available in the room for questions and discussions. In this way, the method can accommodate different learning speeds as well as different levels of previous knowledge and different study backgrounds.

We demonstrate the method using the CL content of a class on Artificial Intelligence in the CS Bachelor's program at Hochschule für Technik Stuttgart as an example. We outline the CL content and describe one class in detail. Student and teacher feedback from this class and two more classes taught through CBL show the method's strengths and its suitedness to all phases of study, be it in the first semester, the final semesters or mid-program.

1 Introduction

Computational Linguistics (CL) integrates methods and levels of description from two disciplines with very different approaches and cultures. In dedicated CL programs, introductory courses on CL are therefore usually taught to heterogeneous groups made up from students of CL programs as well as students from Computer Science (CS), Linguistics, and Language and Communication programs that take CL as a minor subject. Depending on their original field of study, these students have very different previous knowledge and motivation for taking a CL course. This challenges professors to teach concepts from CS to Linguistics students and concepts from Linguistics to CS students without duplicating material that CL students are learning in other classes in their own programs.

A second source of heterogeneity in the student body is differences in students' educational biographies and work experience. This is especially pronounced at Universities of Applied Sciences (Hochschulen für Angewandte Wissenschaften or Fachhochschulen, collectively called HAW hereafter), which have an applied focus, prepare their students primarily for a career in industry and accept students from a large variety of educational backgrounds. At the same time, there are no CL or Linguistics Bachelor's programs at HAW, according to *Hochschulkompass der Hochschulrektorenkonferenz (HRK)* [1], so CL topics are taught primarily to students from CS, Communications, and related programs and usually in program-specific classes.

Despite these structural differences, both at Universities and HAW, the main challenge to teaching introductory topics in CL is heterogeneity in students' previous knowledge and experience (see, for example, Banscherus, 2013). In this situation, learning paths need to be individualized, offering each student the materials they need in order to make the most of the class. This has to be done, however, with a limited amount of teaching staff - especially at HAW, where teaching is done almost exclusively by professors and very little additional teaching staff is available. To address these challenges, a blended learning setting is arguably the most suitable approach (see, for example, Garrison and Kanuka, 2004).

[1] offered by Deutscher Akademischer Austauschdienst: https://www.daad.de/de/studieren-und-forschen-in-deutschland/studienprogramme-sprachkurse/alle-studiengaenge/

Proceedings of the 1st Workshop on Teaching for NLP, pages 19–27
September 18, 2023.

We present the blended-learning method of Computer-based Learning (CBL, Knebusch et al., 2019) which allows students to choose their focus during self-paced learning with frequent feedback through formative tests and with hands-on exercises, while freeing up professors to answer individual questions, give additional input and discuss advanced topics as needed.

We demonstrate the method using the example of an Artificial Intelligence (AI) class which contains a significant amount of CL content and is taught to students in the third semester of the CS Bachelor's program at Hochschule für Technik (HFT) Stuttgart, a HAW. We motivate the selection of the CL-related topics chosen for this class and describe an example session.

We argue for the appropriateness of the method by analysing structured student feedback on this class. Additionally, we discuss professors' impressions and structured student feedback from two other CBL classes taught to demonstrate the versatility of the method across stages of study.

We begin by characterizing teaching at HAW to give some context to the Hochschule für Technik class before introducing the CBL method and the CL content taught in the example class. We finish by discussing student and teacher feedback.

2 Teaching at Universities of Applied Sciences

At HAW, students are heterogeneous with regard to their educational careers and experience: Some matriculate directly after school, others may have work experience in a related field. In accordance with the practical focus of HAW, students are generally interested in and very good at applied work and enjoy project tasks.

Many HAW students are the first academics in their families. This often means that they have little financial support, which can manifest in long commutes to the university and a need to work in parallel to their studies (Bargel and Bargel, 2010). Therefore, students especially value the ability to work on class content independent of the scheduled time and place.

Teaching programs are highly structured and teaching is done almost exclusively by the professors, with little to no support staff. This means that there are no time ressources for providing feedback through grading weekly exercises or for individualized support through many parallel tutorial groups.

3 Method: Computer-based Learning

The main goal of Computer-based learning (CBL, Knebusch et al., 2019) is addressing heterogeneity and providing an optimal learning experience through a tailored and adaptive learning environment. CBL achives this by incorporating times of self-study into the traditional lecture. This is a contrast to the well-known concept of the Inverted Classroom (IC, also known as "flipped classroom"), where students are provided with video lessons to watch in preparation for an in-presence session (Loviscach, 2011).

IC has been shown to support individual learning speeds and pathways, as well as self-directed learning (Dreer, 2008; Lage et al., 2000). However, as the highly-structured curricula at HAW result in a large number of teaching sessions per day for students, implementing a flipped classroom approach for many classes would likely overwhelm the students in terms of required preparation time. Additionally, especially at the beginning of their studies, students may not have developed the self-directed learning skills necessary for the flipped classroom approach.

Instead, CBL mixes instruction and exercises during the scheduled class hours, leveraging live lectures and digital resources such as instructional videos to solidify understanding and bridge knowledge gaps. Moreover, the in-presence setting provides a supportive framework for new students, allowing them to engage in collaborative work, seek guidance from peers, and benefit from expert assistance from instructors. In this way, CBL allows for a high level of individualization while capitalizing on the advantages of face-to-face teaching. Overall, CBL has been shown to promote active learning, maximize students' time spent on task, and facilitate individualized support, leading to improved learning outcomes for first-semester students. (Knebusch et al., 2019)

CBL is best suited for project- or task-based courses, where tasks can be divided into manageable steps. The students work on "Learning Nuggets," which consist of short traditional lecture input, instructional videos, feedback questions, and exercises and apply their new knowledge incrementally to their tasks or projects, transitioning between passive and active learning phases. This approach not only enhances student engagement but also allows for a seamless transition between individual, partner, or group work.

In CBL, assessment and feedback play crucial roles in guiding students' learning journeys. Regular formative assessments, quizzes, and project evaluations are conducted to measure students' progress and provide timely feedback. This feedback helps students identify areas for improvement and adjust their learning strategies accordingly. Additionally, instructors actively engage with students, providing one-on-one discussions to set goals, monitor progress, and offer personalized feedback, thereby supporting students' self-regulation and growth.

CBL was originally developed at HFT Stuttgart as part of the "Qualitätspakt Lehre II" for basic Mathematics courses in engineering programs. Building upon positive evaluation results in Mathematics, we have recently transferred the concept to the CS program, especially in classes for Machine Learning and AI.

3.1 Adapting Existing Materials

When re-framing a traditional class for CBL, existing lecture inputs are broken into shorter learning nuggets and immediately followed by student activities such as self-tests for feedback or matching exercises. Existing materials such as slides and exercises can often be re-used at this step. It is helpful to give (near-)immediate feedback on exercises to help students check their work incrementally during self-study. Self-tests usually have to be created from scratch and will likely require calibration after the first iteration of the class to ensure that the questions work at the desired difficulty level (easy for a comprehension check after a lecture input, harder for practice and exam preparation).

The initial lecture input can be given as a traditional live lecture, but later inputs need to be recorded to provide the self-study input videos. Existing lecture videos can be reused, provided their quality is appropriate. Unfortunately, this is often not the case for pandemic-era lecture captures in our experience, because these tend to be too verbose or to contain errors, delays and interactions with individual students. Video inputs should be concise and to the point, focusing on one specific sub-topic. Since video inputs are generally short (10-15 minutes), a simple screen capture of lecture slides with a voice-over can be used, even though this type of input can be tiring to work through for longer stretches. In sum, re-framing a traditional lecture-and-tutorial setup requires a substantial investment of time and effort, but is not comparable to designing a class from scratch. Also, it is possible to translate only some classes to CBL at first and space out the adaptation over several semesters in this way.

The question of which portions of a class to reframe (and at what speed) can most easily be answered given the professor's reasons for switching to CBL. These will likely be a desire to increase student activity during the lectures, exposure to practical work and involvement with the class. With these in mind, the professor can determine the extent of re-framing needed and prioritise individual classes as needed.

At the same time, on the level of individual lectures, re-framing for CBL is a good opportunity to evaluate the lecture focus on the different aspects of the content and to check the match between lecture inputs and exercises, as well as identifying opportunities for giving students immediate feedback on their progress through tests.

3.2 Evaluating CBL for Advanced Classes

In the process of adapting CBL to instruction in CS, we surmised that CBL is also well suited for more advanced courses, since in later stages of studying, the students already have good self-directed learning and collaborative skills and often prefer working at their own pace. In the following, we will demonstrate the use of CBL for teaching CL content to CS students and evaluate our assumption by reporting student and professor feedback on the use of CBL in three different stages of studies: In the first semester (Mathematics for Civil Engineers), at the beginning of Hauptstudium (third semester, AI for CS) and in an elective module in the final semester of study (Machine Learning and Data Mining for CS). We find evidence that CBL is indeed well-suited for teaching heterogeneous groups throughout the whole study program, new as well as experienced students.

4 Content: Computational Linguistics Topics

At HFT Stuttgart, one opportunity to teach CL to students in the CS Bachelor's program content is as part of a semester-long AI class in students' third semester of study (after completion of the two initial semesters of Grundstudium).

The class uses Russell and Norvig's structuring of the field of AI (Russell and Norvig, 2016), covering topics in "Problem Solving", "Knowledge, reasoning and planning", "Learning" and "Communicating, perceiving and acting". The CL content is covered mostly under this last heading, although some of it also falls under Learning. In detail, the covered topics are

- Introduction to human and human-machine dialogue (Communicating)
- Introduction to morphology and surface normalization (Communicating)
- Text classification with bag-of-words features (Learning)

The topics are chosen in such a way that the students encounter engaging practical tasks and projects and at the same time gain a background understanding of AI techniques that have become ubiquitous in their daily lives. Given the students' existing background in software development and computing, the input is geared towards providing concepts from Linguistics and is intended to demonstrate the complexity of the tasks and the resulting need for careful treatment and analysis of language data.

One topic cluster addresses dialogue and handling of written text, using a tiny Java chat bot[2] and an open-source personal assistant[3] as motivating examples. The students learn about properties of human-human dialogue and expand the chat bot code accordingly, e.g. to cover greetings and appropriately complete other adjacency pairs. Adding functionality to the chat bot motivates additional input about morphology and surface normalization of text and experimentation with existing tools[4]. The Learning task additionally teaches about Machine Learning methodology and treatment of text as training data, both through CBL-based classes and a practical project in which students train a text classifier on a small data set[5].

[2]adapted from `https://www.python-lernen.de/chatbot-programmieren.htm`

[3]Mycroft, `https://mycroft.ai/get-started/`

[4]Students explore GermanNet Rover, `https://weblicht.sfs.uni-tuebingen.de/rover/` and integrate the Mate tools `https://code.google.com/archive/p/mate-tools/wikis/ParserAndModels.wiki` into their chat bot

[5]Data sets change frequently and are chosen from commonly used and publicly available sources, e.g. a subset of the 20 Newsgroups data at `http://qwone.com/~jason/20Newsgroups/` or a subset of the Movie Review Dataset at `https://ai.stanford.edu/~amaas/data/sentiment/`.

5 A Sample Class Session

We now exemplify the CBL method using a class from the Communication segment on dialogue and chat bots, meant for a double session of 2x90 minutes. Table 1 shows the individual components, which we will now discuss one by one.

The class begins with a short, ca. 15 minute introduction to human-machine dialogue followed by an ungraded self-test (administered through the Learning Management System) that is intended to tell students whether they caught all the important concepts or whether they should follow up on some topics, using the lecture slides or asking the professor, before moving on.

In general, the self-tests in CBL give feedback to students about their learning, but also show the professor which concepts larger groups of students may still be unsure of. This helps the professor to address the problem efficiently and quickly by giving a short additional explanation targeted to the exact area of difficulty. Self-tests are ungraded in the AI class in order to stress their informational character.

Once the students are satisfied that they understood the concepts from the introduction, they start on a self-study period by watching a video on the next content input (about human-human dialogue). Students are able to speed up or slow down the video as needed, which is not possible in a live lecture. At this point, students' progress through the materials starts to de-synchronize as some take more time than others on individual tasks.

The video input is followed by two exercises: One on the use of adjacency pairs and evidence of Gricean Maxims (Grice, 1975) in everyday conversations, and an implementation task that asks students to expand the tiny chat bot with correct reactions to e.g., greetings. During this time, the professor is available for questions and discussion. Ideally, the professor cycles through the room during this time in order to be easily available and to lower the threshold for asking for help. This also helps the professor assess the general progress of the class and makes it easier to identify students who work fast and might enjoy an extra challenge or input and students who are struggling.

After the active work on exercises, students switch back to passive mode and watch a video on the technical framework behind automated voice assistants. Students learn about identifying user intentions through matching keywords from the in-

Topic	Activity Format	Work Strategy
Human-machine dialogue	Lecture	Group/Passive
	Self-test	Individual/Active
Human-human dialogue	Video	Individual/Passive
Adjacency pairs and Gricean Maxims	Exercises	Individual/Active
Implementing Adjacency pairs in the chat bot	Exercise	Individual/Active
Automated voice assistants	Video	Individual/Passive
Demo of voice assistant	Lecture	Group/Passive
Intents and skills in the chat bot	Exercise	Pairs/Active
Realistic chat bots	Online Course	Individual/Voluntary

Table 1: Activities in a sample CBL class on Dialogue.

put to *intent* definitions and triggering the matching *skill* to fulfil the request.

This is followed by an interactive live demo of *Mycroft*[6], the sample assistant presented in class. The timing of the group activity can be difficult since student progress is often heterogeneous at this time, but the demo does not presuppose completion of the voice assistant video, so this activity can be paused for the demo.

Finally, the students are asked to use their new knowledge about intents and skills to further extend their chat bot. This task is done in pairs or small groups. One reason for this is to provide variation to the individual work; another reason is didactical: Part of the exercise is the definition of keywords that the chat bot should use to identify the intention of the user (formalised as the *intent*). Students are asked to define their own keywords first and then compare to their partners' solution. For many students, this is an eye-opener to the amount of paraphrase and variation present in natural language interactions. Students are asked to define an intent and the corresponding keywords only, but some students enjoy integrating external APIs and actually implementing the corresponding skill, as well.

With this activity, the class proper is finished. Students who enjoy working on the chat bot are pointed to an external on-line teaching resource[7] that takes them through the construction of a larger chat bot step by step, expanding on the topics covered in the class.

This sample class demonstrates the interleaving of live lectures, video input, self-tests and exercises in CBL. Students regularly switch from active to passive learning modes and from individual to group work while the professor is available for individual interactions as needed. Professors can flexibly add more in-presence lecture phases since they can quickly identify concepts that remain difficult for many students through the self tests. Otherwise, professors' time is mostly spent in individual discussions with their students, which helps them address the heterogeneity of their students' backgrounds efficiently.

6 Student and Professor Perspective

We now go on to report student feedback from a survey taken by CS students in the AI class.

6.1 Structured Feedback by Students

At the end of the semester, we asked the students to complete a survey with a total of 29 questions. Our goal was on the one hand to hear about technical problems with the ressources or issues with the content that had not yet come up. On the other hand, we were interested in the students' reaction to the teaching method. Given the sequence of different activities for each class, we were concerned that students might find it difficult to identify the overarching theme of the classes. Another concern was the use of video inputs, since in the aftermath of pandmic-related on-line teaching students commented that they were fed up with recorded content. Therefore, we wanted to know whether the students felt they were getting appropriate amounts of interaction with their professor given the large amount of self-study activities and whether they were able to focus during the vidoes. Finally, we asked whether the students felt prompted to dig deeper into the materials by the test and exercise activities, as intended by the method.

Fig. 1 shows the results of the survey, omitting questions on technical and content quality. 22 students (41% of the total number of actively participating students) took part in the on-line survey, which was announced in class and by email.

We find that students overwhelmingly reported

[6] `https://mycroft.ai/get-started/`

[7] `https://ki-campus.org/courses/conversational-ai`

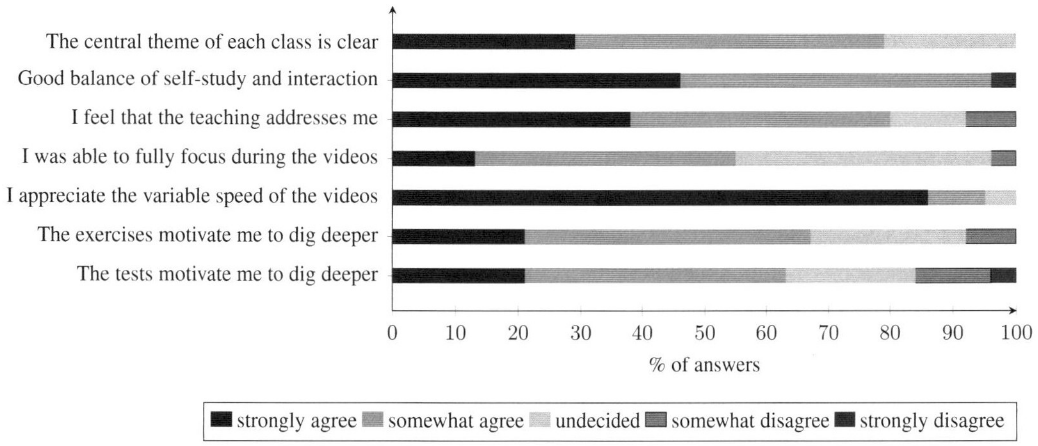

Figure 1: Student feedback on CBL from third-semester CS students. $N = 24$, or 42% of enrolled students.

no or few issues identifying the overall theme of all the activities in a class (21% were undecided). They were therefore able to follow the train of thought of the materials.

Students were very or at least somewhat satisfied with the balance between self-study and interaction with the professor. 4% or two out of 22 students however strongly disagreed, indicating some potential for polarization. Similarly, 80% of students felt personally addressed by the teaching method, while the rest were undecided or somewhat disagreed. Overall, it appears that the method appealed to the majority of students, but there was a small and vocal group that disliked the approach. We do not have numbers for comparison to other teaching methods like lectures or classic tutorial sessions for comparison, unfortunately.

Regarding the use of videos, almost half of students report that they found it hard to fully focus on the input. Again, we have no comparison to a traditional lecture to gauge how much of this issue is due to the frontal lecture paradigm and how much is due to the specific CBL setup where the students' neighbors may simultaneously be working on other activities. We also include an intriguing piece of feedback on the video materials: Students greatly appreciate the possibility of speeding up the video replay, something that is not possible in a traditional lecture, of course. This encourages us to overall recommend the continued use of videos in CBL (over live lecture inputs, which are also hard to time as the class proceeds).

Finally, the self-test feedback and exercises motivated the majority of students to engage more deeply with the learning materials. Feedback on the tests is more contentious than on the exercises, which may be due to the nature of the self-tests: They were intended as a quick way of checking whether students remembered the main points of the lecture and video inputs and may therefore have been too easy to be challenging for the majority of engaged learners. We plan to experiment with the use of adaptive testing for the feedback tests in order to present each student individually with questions that are appropriate for their level.

The relatively low participation in the survey (of less than 50% of the students who actively participate in the class) correlates with attendance and may be explained by a tendency of students to choose different times and places to work through the material, even if the professor is not available then. After a week, the tests and exercises routinely show more active users than students were present in class. We see this as a further advantage of the method, since it offers flexibility to students and allows them to work independently, taking charge of their own learning goals despite the usually highly structured HAW study programs.

In sum, the picture is positive: students feel addressed personally through CBL and feel motivated to engage with the materials by the self-tests and exercises. Even though the method was developed for beginning students, students in the middle of their study program also appreciate CBL and its advantages (for example, the variable speed of videos or the option of working through the materials whenever and wherever convenient). We did not see students confused by the large number of activities per class or feeling left on their own with self-study activities. Students did, however, report that they had a hard time focussing on the videos, so these will be revised for length and conciseness. Overall, we conclude that CBL is an appropriate method for teaching CL content to a heterogenous set of students. We now go on to further demonstrate the versatility of CBL by feedback from students in the very first and last semesters of their study programs.

6.2 Structured Feedback from Other Classes

When transferring CBL from first-semester courses in Mathematics to CS topics, we also expanded to classes from other phases of the study program: AI (as just discussed Section 6.1) in the third semester and a class on Machine Learning in students' final semester. We collected structured feedback from all three courses using the same questionnaire in order to be able to compare students' impressions and see how well the method adapts to the different needs of students at different points in their studies.

Fig. 2 shows the feedback from the first-semester students (Civil Engineering program, Mathematics class) at the top and the feedback from the final-semester students (CS, Machine Learning) at the bottom. In the middle, we repeat the feedback from the third-semester AI students (cf. Section 6.1) for comparison.

Our first finding is that students in all phases of study are generally satisfied with CBL: in every group, at least 75% of students strongly agree or somewhat agree with the first three of our feedback propositions. Students in higher semesters are at least as satisfied as first-semester students, for whom the method was developed. This is proof of the versatility of the method and ties in well with earlier findings (Knebusch et al., 2019).

Additionally, interesting patterns emerge across semesters: As students progress in their studies, they have an easier time identifying the central theme of each class and are more satisfied with the mix of self-study and interaction in CBL. They also feel more personally addressed by the teaching method (evidenced by far less disagreement with our third proposition and a higher percentage of strong agreement with it). We interpret this as a sign of students' increased experience with the HAW learning environment and better self-directed learning skills. More experienced students are more comfortable during self-study than the inexperienced first-semester students, and also report an easier time focusing on the videos as the semesters progress. They seem to have developed more sophisticated strategies for dealing with video materials, as the third-semester and higher students express much more appreciation for the variable video speeds than the first semester students.

The final two feedback propositions ask about the exercises and tests. Here, the third-semester AI students are least motivated by the exercises, possibly because they also complete a group project for their class, which does not exist in the first-semester Mathematics class and which is larger than the corresponding Machine Learning group project. At the same time, the results are reason to scrutinize the AI materials more closely. The large positive impact of the tests for the first-semester students in Mathematics can be explained by the more challenging nature of the tests in their class (cf. Section 6.1).

In sum, we find that students from all phases of study appreciate CBL, but we see that the increased self-study skills of higher-semester students serve them well. The participation rate in the feedback speaks a similar language: 78% of first-semester students participated, but only about 40% of students in higher semesters. This is correlated with attendance rates (although all students were invited to participate) and demonstrates that students in later semesters appreciate the option of using the CBL materials entirely for self-study. We conclude that CBL can be flexibly used for classes throughout a study program, since it offers guidance to inexperienced students and flexibility to advanced students in addition to maximising individualized learning and individual interaction with the professor if desired.

6.3 Impressions from Professors

The authors have taught the above-mentioned classes using CBL. Our informal observations on CBL classes are very positive. Students are engaged and active during the whole of class, and much more so than during traditional lectures or even the introductory lecture part. During exercises, often small groups form spontaneously as students explain the tasks to each other and discuss them. The atmosphere in class is very focused and students rarely engage in non-class related activities even in 2x90 minute segments.

We also appreciate the opportunity to interact with individual students and discuss difficult issues face-to-face instead of lecturing to a group. The

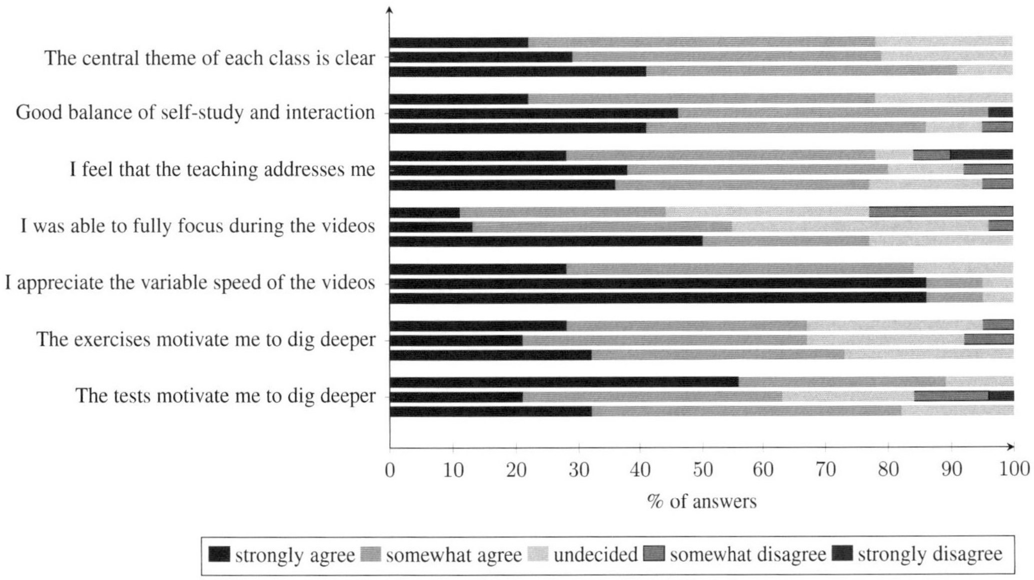

Figure 2: Student feedback on CBL. Top: First-semester Civil Engineering students in Mathematics ($N = 18$, or 78% of enrolled students.), middle: third-semester CS students in AI ($N = 24$, or 42% of enrolled students), bottom: final-semester CS students in Machine Learning ($N = 22$, or 41% of enrolled students).

self-study activities in CBL also free up time for more in-depth discussions with students who already have some experience with the class topic and who otherwise might be bored by the materials and disengage with the class.

7 Conclusions

We have presented the adaptation of the CBL method (Knebusch et al., 2019) to teaching CL content to CS students on the Bachelor's level. CBL encourages self-study in the presence of the professor, who is available for questions and discussions. It therefore helps to address heterogeneity in students' educational backgrounds and previous experience, frees up professors to interact with individual students and provides students with a large amount of hands-on exercises.

Structured feedback from students show that they feel personally addressed by the method and appreciate the balance between self-study and interaction with the professor. The materials motivate them to deeply engage with the learning materials and they appreciate the ability to e.g. choose the speed of input videos according to their needs.

The structured feedback from first-semester, third-semester and final-semester students also demonstrates that all groups profit from CBL, while the more experienced students make use of the flexibility afforded by the focus on self-study. Anecdotal evidence from professors shows consistent student engagement with the materials and the ability to cater to individual students, be they struggling or advanced.

In sum, we present evidence that the method is very suitable for teaching with a focus on addressing heterogeneity in different study programs and at various stages during study programs. We therefore believe that the method has proven its versatility and can be used in other academic settings where heterogeneity is present in the student body - for example teaching CL to groups made up of students from various fields.

References

Ulf Banscherus. 2013. *Erfahrungen mit der Konzeption und Durchführung von Nachfrage- und Bedarfsanalysen für Angebote der Hochschulweiterbildung: ein Überblick*, volume 7 of *Thematischer Bericht der wissenschaftlichen Begleitung des Bund-Länder-Wettbewerbs "Aufstieg durch Bildung: offene Hochschulen"*.

Holger Bargel and Tino Bargel. 2010. Ungleichheiten und Benachteiligungen im Hochschulstudium aufgrund der sozialen Herkunft der Studierenden.

Silvia Dreer. 2008. E-Learning als Möglichkeit zur Unterstützung des selbstgesteuerten Lernens an Berufsschulen. *Zeitschrift für Theorie und Praxis der Medienbildung*, pages 1–25.

D. Randy Garrison and Heather Kanuka. 2004. Blended learning – Uncovering its transformative potential in higher education. *The Internet and Higher Education*, 2:95–105.

Paul Grice. 1975. Logic and conversation. In P. Cole and . J Morgan, editors, *Syntax and Semantics*, volume 3, pages 41–58. Academic Press, New York.

Anselm Knebusch, Anke Pfeiffer, and Michael Wandler. 2019. Individualisiertes Lernen mit Computer begleitetem Lernen (Individualized learning with computer-assisted learning). *Zeitschrift für Hochschulentwicklung*, 14:153–170.

Maureen J. Lage, Glenn J. Platt, and Treglia Michael. 2000. Inverting the classroom: A gateway to creating an inclusive learning environment. *The Journal of Economic Education*, 31:30–43.

Jörn Loviscach. 2011. Mathematik auf YouTube: Herausforderungen, Werkzeuge, Erfahrungen. In *DeLFI 2011 - Die 9. e-Learning Fachtagung Informatik*, pages 91–102, Bonn. Gesellschaft für Informatik e.V.

Stuart Russell and Peter Norvig. 2016. *Artificial Intelligence: A modern approach*. Pearson International.

QUEST: Quizzes Utilizing Engaging StoryTelling

Thomas Arnold
Ubiquitous Knowledge Processing Lab (UKP Lab)
Department of Computer Science and Hessian Center for AI (hessian.AI)
Technical University of Darmstadt
www.ukp.tu-darmstadt.de

Abstract

The support of motivation and engagement during lectures holds significant importance in teaching. In this study, we introduce a gamified quiz-based classroom approach, denoted as *QUEST: Quizzes Utilizing Engaging StoryTelling*, to tackle these challenges. Our approach utilizes immersive quiz templates within a competitive environment. We conduct an experimental study, comparing the course evaluations of semesters with no quizzes, standard quizzes, and the QUEST approach. Consistent with theoretical expectations, the feedback demonstrates a positive impact of gamified in-class activities on intrinsic motivation and continuous learning. Our analysis of the feedback presents the initial evidence supporting the positive effects of QUEST in NLP teaching. All quizzes will be openly accessible for free usage[1].

1 Introduction

Behold, the earth is attacked by an evil force of infernal, NLP energy: THE LEMMATIZER! If you want to know how unlemmatized catch-phrases can save the earth, see Figure 1.

In recent years, the importance of high-quality teaching has escalated, and the emergence of generative AI tools has reignited the discussion on desired learning objectives for students across various educational levels. Moreover, the availability of hybrid or online-only courses has introduced numerous advantages for students, such as the flexibility to learn at their own pace, independent of time and location. However, this mode of instruction also amplifies certain inherent challenges in the learning process, including the maintenance of self-motivation and sustained engagement in continuous learning. To progress effectively through the course material, students must exercise significant discipline and overcome hurdles like self-motivation. While AI-driven tools have their benefits, it is essential to acknowledge that their use presents some pedagogical concerns. As pointed out in a relevant study (Churchill, 2023), utilizing such tools may diminish the depth of engagement with the subject matter. Engaged learning typically involves researching a topic, seeking information, summarizing knowledge, evaluating debates, considering different viewpoints, and forming one's own opinion—an immersive learning experience that may be forfeited when relying heavily on AI tools. In light of these observations, it becomes increasingly necessary to explore innovative approaches and concepts to effectively address the challenges brought about by this new educational landscape.

In the research literature, one concept that plays a significant role in promoting self-motivated and continuous learning is gamification. The idea is to incorporate elements of game design into a non-gaming educational context to enhance learning and intrinsic motivation (Bai et al., 2020). This concept can be applied to quizzes, serving as a starting point for implementing gamification in teaching. Quizzes can provide immediate feedback on tasks, contributing to intrinsic motivation through the use of points and leaderboards (Rigby and Ryan, 2011). Additionally, quizzes can enhance overall course activity by offering time-dependent quiz sessions that allow students to earn points and achieve a higher class rank (Sailer and Sailer, 2021). Quiz systems like Mentimeter (https://www.mentimeter.com) are built on these functionalities, offering live quizzes with points and leaderboards, encouraging participants

[1] https://github.com/UKPLab/QUEST

Proceedings of the 1st Workshop on Teaching for NLP, pages 28–36
September 18, 2023.

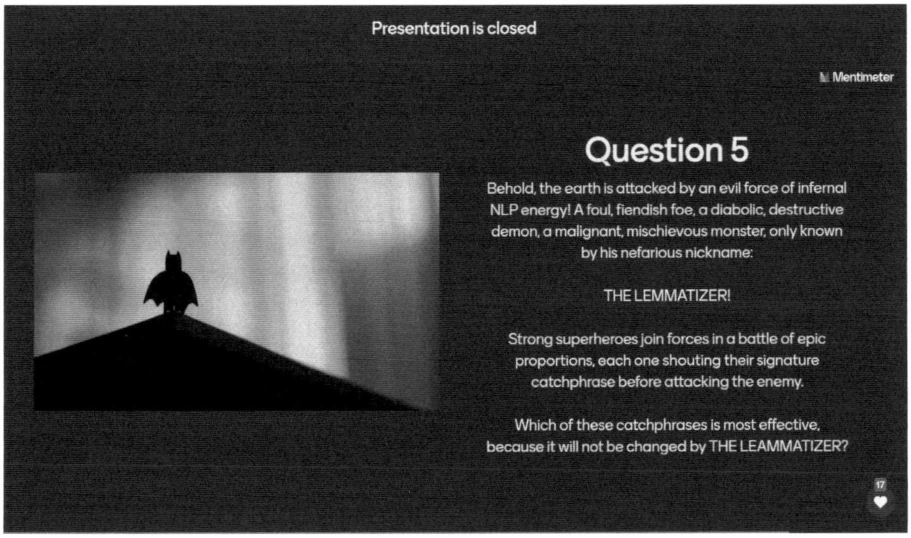

Figure 1: An example question on the topic of lemmatization. Is it A: "I am Groot", B: "Up, up, and away!", C: "Avengers, assemble!" or D: "It's morphing time!"? Read the discussion section for the correct answer!

to earn points by being both correct and fast. Sailer and Sailer (2021) demonstrated that such gamified quizzes can enhance motivation and application-oriented knowledge.

Although these quizzes show promise in addressing the aspects of self-motivated and continuous learning, they are not yet widely utilized in NLP teaching. However, apart from these quiz elements, there is another aspect that can foster motivation and engagement: storytelling. Storytelling enhances learning and classroom engagement by capturing students' interest and immersing them in the narrative (Lugmayr et al., 2017). Arsenijevic et al. (2016) emphasized the importance of storytelling in understanding the content. Despite its relevance, storytelling remains relatively unfamiliar in the context of teaching.

To address these research and teaching gaps, we introduce `QUEST`, `Quizzes Utilizing Engaging StoryTelling`. The core idea of `QUEST` is to offer a method of intrinsically motivating students to stay actively engaged and develop multiple competencies in a gamified in-person or online learning environment. We utilize Mentimeter quizzes with immersive storytelling. In this study, we showcase the implementation of `QUEST` in two NLP courses and present the feedback we received from our students. Through our analysis of feedback, we compare the responses received over many years (2018 - 2022). In 2018, we did not employ quizzes at all. In contrast, we used quizzes without gaming elements and storytelling in 2019. Finally, beginning in 2020, we implemented `QUEST`. Our analysis of feedback reveals positive responses from students regarding self-motivation and continuous learning. Moreover, we find that students perceive the content as more comprehensible overall compared to previous years. Our results demonstrate an initial positive trend that will require further examination in the future. However, without a detailed systematic evaluation of `QUEST` across multiple semesters, we cannot conclude a universally positive effect. We provide all quiz templates and encourage the adoption of `QUEST` in as many in-person or online courses as possible, as this will help us gain a better understanding of its positive effects.

2 Related Work

`QUEST` integrates various learning elements to enhance the NLP learning environment. In this section, we will introduce the three fundamental concepts of `QUEST`: Gamification, Quizzes, and Storytelling.

Gamification. Gamification involves incorporating game design elements into non-game contexts (Deterding et al., 2011; Nieto-Escamez and Roldán-Tapia, 2021). It has been applied and studied in educational settings, showing positive effects on learning and motivation (Seaborn and Fels, 2015; Bai et al., 2020; Sailer and Homner, 2020). However, further research is needed to explore these effects, particularly in higher education (Huang and Hew, 2018; Sailer and Sailer, 2021). The application of gamification in NLP teaching remains relatively unexplored (van Halteren, 2002).

Quizzes. Quizzes are often used as a starting point for implementing gamification in teaching and learning environments (Sailer and Sailer, 2021). They provide immediate feedback at the task level through point-based scoring, which has the potential to enhance performance and learning (Hattie and Timperley, 2007; Kulik and Kulik, 1988). Quizzes can also facilitate competitive or cooperative interactions among learners, typically through leaderboards, which aligns with gamification strategies (Sailer and Sailer, 2021).

The self-determination theory explains the motivational appeal of game design elements, and it has been applied in gamification studies (Sailer and Sailer, 2021; Mekler et al., 2017). This theory highlights three psychological needs crucial for intrinsic motivation and high-quality learning: competence, autonomy, and social relatedness (Ryan and Deci, 2000). In the context of gamified quizzes, competence and social relatedness are particularly relevant (Vansteenkiste and Ryan, 2013). Competence can be addressed through feedback mechanisms, such as point systems in gamified quizzes (Rigby and Ryan, 2011). Social relatedness can be fostered through shared goals, like team leaderboards in gamified quizzes (Sailer et al., 2017).

(Serious) Storytelling. Stories have long been used to communicate ideas and knowledge, serving both immersive and informational purposes (Davenport and Prusak, 1998; Arsenijevic et al., 2016). Serious storytelling, introduced by (Lugmayr et al., 2017), refers to storytelling with a purpose beyond entertainment. It has gained popularity as a method for formal education (Collins, 1999). Storytelling enhances understanding and overall in-class activity, aligning with Bloom's taxonomy of learning outcomes (Arsenijevic et al., 2016; Lugmayr et al., 2017).

Story-Telling Gamified Quizzes in NLP Teaching. The integration of these concepts presents a novel approach to NLP teaching. To the best of our knowledge, no existing approach combines these elements. `QUEST` serves as a starting point for implementing story-driven gamification elements in NLP teaching.

3 Course Background

We implemented `QUEST` in two courses from the curriculum offered by the Ubiquitous Knowledge Engineering Lab at the Technical University (TU) of Darmstadt:

The course titled *Natural Language Processing and the Web* primarily targets M.Sc.-level students in computer science. However, its interdisciplinary nature also attracts students from other fields such as linguistic and literary computing or psychology in IT. Since its inception in the 2008/2009 academic year, the course content has undergone regular revisions to incorporate current trends in NLP research and emerging web technologies, including Information Retrieval, Argumentation Mining, and Question Answering techniques. Additionally, the course provides a brief introduction to fundamental NLP analysis levels. Over the years, the course's enrollment has steadily increased, with the current iteration attracting up to 200 students.

In contrast, *Information Management* is a course for B.Sc. computer science students. It involves foundations of structured data processing through relational databases and managing unstructured, textual data sourced by utilizing basic methods of Natural Language Processing. Since this is a mandatory course in the computer science curriculum, the course size is much larger, with up to 700 students per semester.

4 Method

We started implementing `QUEST`, which involves thematic activities with story-driven tests, in our course Natural Language Processing and the Web during the past five winter semesters: 2018/2019 - 2022/2023. In the first year, we conducted simple interactive quizzes using the live feedback tool PINGO. PINGO allowed us to prepare sets of questions with various formats (e.g., single-choice, multiple-choice, numeric, textual) and display them to students during the lecture. Students could answer the questions using their own devices, and the results were presented to the audience. The purpose of these quizzes was to:

- activate the students
- reiterate knowledge from previous lectures
- emphasize important aspects of the current lecture
- provide example questions for exam preparation

Starting from the 2019/2020 semester, we introduced QUEST in this course as an advanced, gamified version of interactive quizzes with creative, story-driven scenarios. In the course Information Management, we started the implementation of QUEST in the summer semester of 2021 and used it in every session in 2022. We use the live feedback platform Mentimeter as an online tool, which enables the integration of interactive polls resembling modern quiz game shows. Participants are presented with up to five questions that they can answer using their devices. Each participant enters the quiz with a randomly assigned icon and alias. In this format, participants are not only motivated to provide correct answers but also to answer quickly, as points are awarded based on both correctness and response time. After each question, a leaderboard showing the top ten participants is displayed, creating a competitive and dynamic environment.

To further enhance student engagement, we present all questions in the form of narrations with story-driven scenarios. For instance, instead of directly asking about the advantages of Support Vector Machines, we frame the question within a fictional contest called "Machine Learning's Next Top Model," where the contestant "Support Vector Machine" is introduced and commented on by the jury. This approach aims to promote out-of-the-box thinking and provide an enjoyable learning experience. Figure 1 illustrates an example of such a question, and Figure 2 shows the core slide template used for these interactive quizzes.

This form of gamified, creative quizzes was created with regard to these additional goals:

- increasing student participation
- enhancing motivation through competition
- introducing gamification for the positive effect of fun on motivation
- enable out-of-the-box thinking by using story-driven scenarios

5 Evaluation

Quantitative Feedback. After each iteration of our courses, the participating students are asked to fill out anonymous evaluation questionnaires to express their opinion. These questionnaires are standardized for all lectures at the TU Darmstadt and were not conducted specifically for this study.

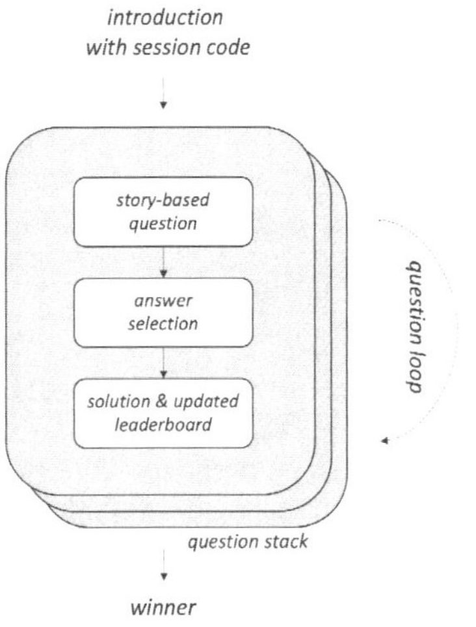

Figure 2: Overview of core slide template. The question loop is included once per question.

The evaluations include questions about the lecturer, the room, organizational issues, and the contents of the lectures. We include feedback from four years of the lecture - one year before interactive quizzes were introduced and the three years of our involvement. It is important to note that all numbers and written feedback depend on various variables, including the lecturing staff, slight changes in lecture content, or the actual cohort of students. Therefore, we present this feedback as a correlation with the effects of our method, rather than claiming causality.

In contrast to our Master's lecture, *Information Management* is much larger. As a result, the evaluation results are much more meaningful and representative, with about 70 - 100 evaluations submitted each semester compared to 10 - 20 in *Natural Language Processing and the Web*. Most of the questions in the standardized questionnaire are in Likert Scale format, where participants express their opinion on given statements on a five-level range. From all the questions in the questionnaire, only a small subset is relevant to this study. The distribution of the evaluation values from the last three years of our *Information Management* lecture can be seen in Figure 3. We tested the statistical significance of the effects using chi-square tests ($p < 0.05$).

The motivation to learn outside of the course shows a statistically significant increase with the integration of QUEST. As indicated by the qualitative feedback, students feel self-motivated by the

w/o QUIZ
Could be improved by... Include a few quizzes in between. These help to prepare for the exam.
Could be improved by... More material for exam preparation. Largely unclear what the exam will look like.
Could be improved by... Adding interactive elements. Lecture is a bit dry.
PINGO QUIZ
I liked ... Pingo sections were awesome and are a great way to feel more prepared for the exam
I liked... The use of pingo, though it could be more ;)
I liked... Using pingo as an effective tool to deepen understanding, provide a fun little break from the lecture and give examples for the lecture
Could be improved by... more pingo
`Quizzes Utilizing Engaging StoryTelling`
The lecturer was outstanding... use of novel technologies such as the quiz system with the score ranking - combines fun and educational purposes
I liked... Mentimenter even motivated me to prepare for the lecture so that I could answer the questions well.
I liked... The digital quizzes held by Thomas were really entertaining and educational
I liked... The creativity Mr. Arnold probably spent on the surveys was very motivating and engaging. Also, the sometimes humorous examples/explanations often made algorithms or concepts very clear and easy to understand.
I liked... The live lectures were very good. The quizzes made it easier to concentrate and focus on the later parts of the lecture. MentiMeter especially was really fun!
The lecturer was outstanding because... The quizzes are a good way to self-examine, and the stories and built-in jokes also build an emotional connection to the material.
The lecturer was outstanding because... Online teaching is as dry as the Sahara, but Mr. Arnold did an amazing job to make the lecture more fun and provide opportunities for interaction and critical thinking.
The lecturer was outstanding because... The interactive parts during the lecture were great and vastly improved my willingness to participate and attend the lectures, as well as the information gain.

Table 1: Feedback from the university evaluation addressing interactive elements and the quizzes.

regular quizzes, and some even go to great lengths to prepare for them, which indicates improved continuous learning. The perceived effective usage of interactive platforms also reached its peak when quizzes were first implemented. In addition, we observe positive trends in the perception of clear learning objectives and the integration of theory and practice for the years when interactive quizzes were implemented. This suggests the potential benefits of practical, interactive tests during the learning process. Overall, adding `QUEST` has had a statistically significant, positive effect on course evaluations, as evidenced by the higher overall grades and the increase in teaching award proposals.

Qualitative Feedback. While the questionnaires primarily focus on simpler Likert Scale evaluations, the set of questions allowing free-form answers is better suited to draw direct conclusions between our methods and the perceived sentiment. The included questions that can be answered in free textual format are: "About the course, I liked very much...", "Next time, the course could be improved by...", and "I would recommend the lecturer for a prize for outstanding teaching because...". Table 1 contains submitted feedback related to interactive unit usage (or lack thereof).

Prior to the implementation of interactive quizzes in the classroom, students expressed that quizzes could be helpful, especially for exam prepa-

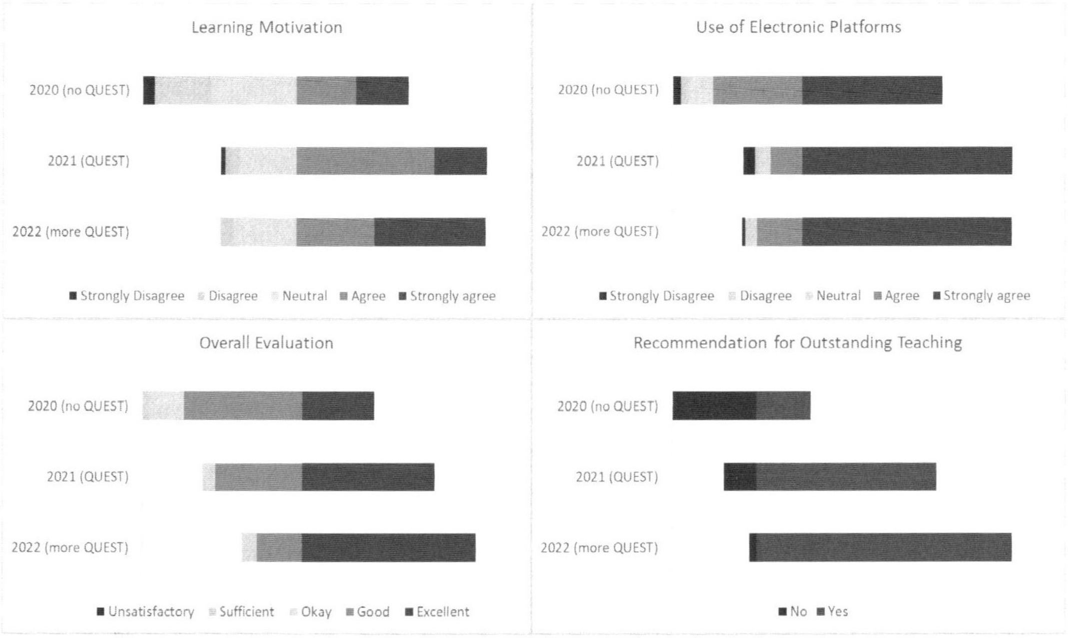

Figure 3: *Information Management* students' evaluations of three years to the questions "The learning objectives of the course were made clear", "The lecturer used electronic platforms effectively", "What total grade do you give this lecture?" and "I would recommend the lecturer for a price for outstanding teaching". QUEST was introduced to this lecture in 2021, and used in all sessions in 2022.

ration. This need is directly reflected in the feedback on PINGO quizzes, where students stated that they were "a great way to feel prepared for the exam". In addition, PINGO was perceived as an "effective tool to deepen understanding" and provide "fun little breaks". The majority of students appreciated the use of interactive quizzes, with Mentimeter quizzes receiving particular praise for their entertainment value and educational benefits. The quizzes were commended for making the lectures more engaging, motivating students to prepare and participate actively, and providing clear explanations of algorithms and concepts. Incorporating novel technologies and the creativity displayed in the quizzes were also highlighted as positive aspects. Students mentioned that these quizzes "combine fun and educational purposes" and "vastly improved my willingness to participate and attend the lectures, as well as information gain". One student mentioned that an announced quiz motivated them "to prepare for the lecture so I could answer the questions well". All this positive feedback indicates increased participation by students and enhanced motivation caused by our quizzes.

QUEST questionnaire. In the 2021 edition of our course *Information Management*, we developed a specialized questionnaire to assess the extent and perceived benefits of QUEST. Our aim was to determine which factor - the competitive aspect of quizzes, the storytelling element, or the gamified presentation - has the greatest influence on motivation and learning. Additionally, we wanted to investigate if there are students who have reservations about any of these aspects or feel distracted by them. The results of the evaluation offer valuable insights into students' opinions and experiences with the quizzes used in the lecture. An overview of the evaluation results can be found in Figure 4. The complete results of this evaluation are available in our shared repository.

Regarding the overall opinion on the quizzes, a substantial number of students expressed positive views. A majority of 103 students (out of the total 108 respondents) indicated that they were at least looking forward to the quizzes, demonstrating a high level of anticipation. Only a small number of students found the quizzes to be acceptable or disliked them. Similarly, only 1 student would have preferred to skip the quizzes.

When comparing the motivation during the quizzes to regular tests, a clear trend emerges. A total of 35 students felt more motivated during the quizzes, while an even larger number of 58 students reported higher motivation levels. On the

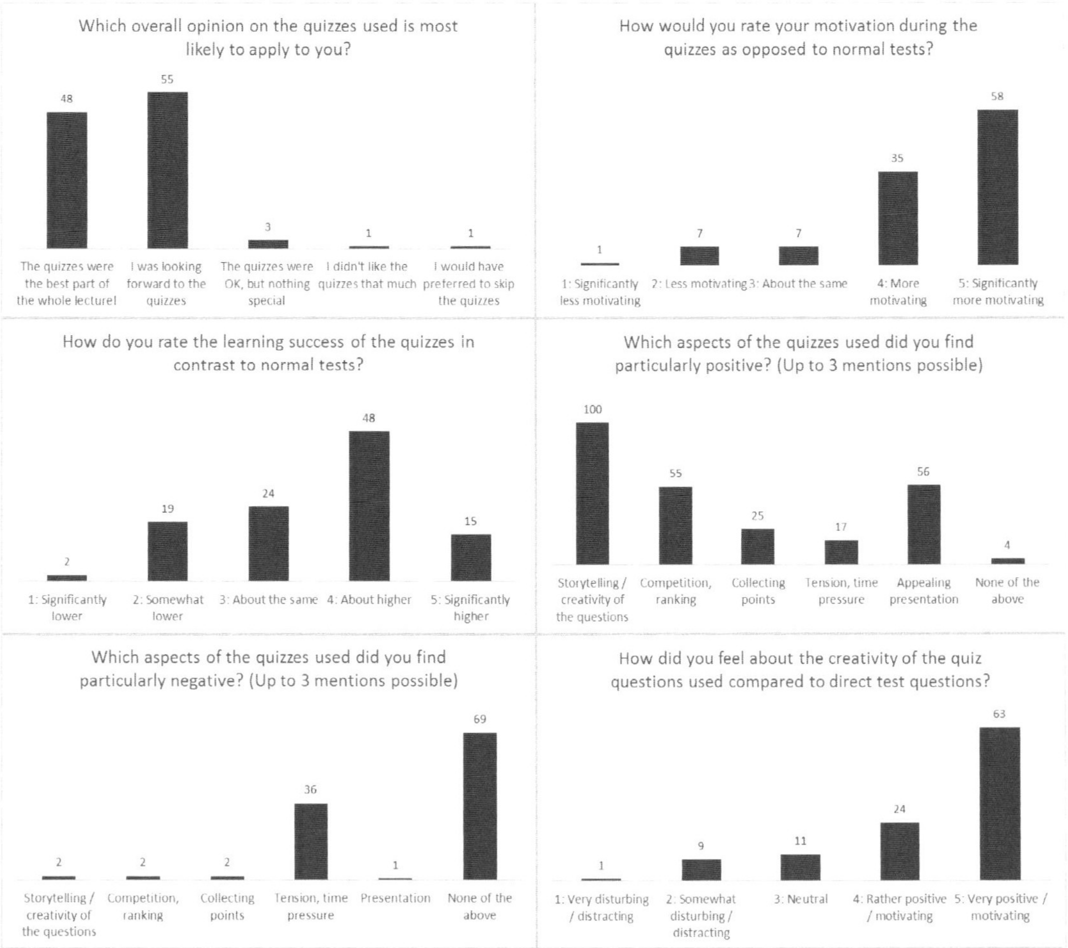

Figure 4: Results of the QUEST evaluation with 108 answers from *Information Management* students of 2021. All participants gave their consent to use and publish the anonymized data.

other hand, 7 students felt less motivated, and only 1 student stated a notable decrease in motivation during the quizzes.

In terms of learning success, the majority of students felt that the quizzes were effective. A total of 48 students believed that the quizzes resulted in higher learning success compared to regular tests, with 15 students even stating that the learning success was considerably higher. While 19 students felt the quizzes had somewhat lower learning success, only 2 students thought the learning success was significantly lower.

Analyzing the aspects of the quizzes that students found particularly positive, a few noteworthy factors emerged. The storytelling/creativity of the questions received the highest number of mentions, with 100 students appreciating this aspect. The competitive and ranking aspect was also well-received by 55 students. Additionally, 56 students found the appealing presentation of the quizzes to be a positive aspect.

When considering the aspects of the quizzes that students found particularly negative, the tension and time pressure associated with the quizzes were perceived negatively by 36 students, making it the most frequently mentioned negative aspect. Remarkably, a majority of 69 students did not find any of the mentioned aspects to be negative.

Examining the students' perception of the creativity of the quiz questions compared to direct test questions, a considerable number of students expressed positive views. 63 students found the creativity of the quiz questions to be very positive and motivating, while 24 students had a generally positive perception. Only 1 and 9 students, respectively, found the creativity of the quiz questions to be either disturbing or distracting.

6 Discussion

We implemented and validated the use of our approach, called QUEST: Quizzes Utilizing Engaging StoryTelling, in two NLP lectures over a five-year period. Due to the number of factors that changed during this time, it is challenging to establish a direct correlation between our method and increased student motivation or learning success. However, the evaluation questionnaires indicate trends of enhanced self-motivation and clearer learning objectives. These trends are further supported by positive feedback from students, emphasizing the advantages of quizzes in terms of motivation, engagement, and exam preparation.

Based on the questionnaire results, several conclusions can be drawn regarding the use of quizzes in the lecture and the overall effectiveness of the QUEST method:

- **Positive reception:** The majority of students expressed positive opinions about the quizzes used in the lecture. A significant number of students considered the quizzes to be the best part of the whole lecture and looked forward to them. This indicates that quizzes can be an engaging and enjoyable component of the learning experience.

- **Increased motivation:** A substantial number of students reported higher motivation levels during the quizzes compared to normal tests. This suggests that the competitive aspect, storytelling element, and gamified presentation employed in the quizzes contributed to increased student motivation. The quizzes provided a more stimulating and engaging learning environment, motivating students to actively participate.

- **Improved learning success:** A significant proportion of students believed that the quizzes led to higher learning success compared to traditional tests. This indicates that the QUEST teaching method, with its emphasis on quizzes, facilitated effective learning outcomes. The combination of engaging elements such as storytelling and competition potentially contributed to a deeper understanding and retention of the course material.

- **Positive aspects:** The storytelling/creativity of the quiz questions and the competitive nature of the quizzes were identified as major positive aspects.

- **Negative aspects:** Some students expressed concerns about the tension and time pressure associated with the quizzes.

- **Varied preferences:** Individual preferences regarding the quizzes varied among students, emphasizing the importance of flexibility in teaching methods.

Overall, the evaluation results suggest that the use of quizzes, combined with elements such as storytelling, competition, and appealing presentation, can significantly contribute to student motivation and learning success. However, it's essential to consider the potential negative aspects, such as tension and time pressure, and tailor the quizzes to accommodate different student preferences and learning styles. These conclusions provide valuable insights for further refining and improving the QUEST teaching method in future iterations of our courses.

Moving forward, we aim to expand the application of QUEST to other lectures within our group, as well as adjacent courses. Additionally, we plan to explore the potential transferability of this method to other fields of study. To facilitate the implementation of quizzes in in-person or online classroom environments, we intend to create detailed guidelines with best practices. Furthermore, we seek to gather helpful advice on the creative process behind our set of story-driven questions to support the creation of new quiz content.

We have already received positive feedback from other lecturers who expressed interest in reusing the QUEST template, question structures, or a set of questions suitable for their own lectures. All QUEST resources, including templates, questions, and further information, are openly shared in a repository[2].

Finally, the `correct answer` for our example question is `B`.
The catchphrase "Up, up, and away" is the only one that is not changed by lemmatization. Were you able to save the earth?

[2] https://github.com/UKPLab/QUEST

References

Olja Arsenijevic, Dragan Trivan, and Milan Milosevic. 2016. Storytelling as a Modern Tool of Construction of Information Security Corporate Culture. *Ekonomika, Journal for Economic Theory and Practice and Social Issues*, 62(4).

Shurui Bai, Khe Foon Hew, and Biyun Huang. 2020. Does gamification improve student learning outcome? Evidence from a meta-analysis and synthesis of qualitative data in educational contexts. *Educational Research Review*, 30:100322.

Elizabeth F. Churchill. 2023. Throwing spaghetti against the wall: Why technology leaders need to invest more in hci and ux. *Interactions*, 30(3):21–22.

Fiona Collins. 1999. The Use of Traditional Storytelling in Education to the Learning of Literacy Skills. *Early Child Development and Care*, 152(1):77–108.

Thomas Davenport and Laurence Prusak. 1998. *Working Knowledge: How Organizations Manage What They Know*, volume 1.

Sebastian Deterding, Dan Dixon, Rilla Khaled, and Lennart Nacke. 2011. From game design elements to gamefulness. In *Proceedings of the 15th International Academic MindTrek Conference on Envisioning Future Media Environments - MindTrek '11*, page 9, New York, New York, USA. ACM Press.

John Hattie and Helen Timperley. 2007. The Power of Feedback. *Review of Educational Research*, 77(1):81–112.

Biyun Huang and Khe Foon Hew. 2018. Implementing a theory-driven gamification model in higher education flipped courses: Effects on out-of-class activity completion and quality of artifacts. *Computers & Education*, 125:254–272.

James A. Kulik and Chen-Lin C. Kulik. 1988. Timing of Feedback and Verbal Learning. *Review of Educational Research*, 58(1):79.

Artur Lugmayr, Erkki Sutinen, Jarkko Suhonen, Carolina Islas Sedano, Helmut Hlavacs, and Calkin Suero Montero. 2017. Serious storytelling – a first definition and review. *Multimedia Tools and Applications*, 76(14):15707–15733.

Elisa D. Mekler, Florian Brühlmann, Alexandre N. Tuch, and Klaus Opwis. 2017. Towards understanding the effects of individual gamification elements on intrinsic motivation and performance. *Computers in Human Behavior*, 71:525–534.

Francisco Antonio Nieto-Escamez and María Dolores Roldán-Tapia. 2021. Gamification as online teaching strategy during covid-19: A mini-review. *Frontiers in Psychology*, 12.

Scott Rigby and Richard M. Ryan. 2011. *Glued to games : how video games draw us in and hold us spellbound.* ABC-CLIO, Santa Barbara, CA.

Richard M. Ryan and Edward L. Deci. 2000. Intrinsic and Extrinsic Motivations: Classic Definitions and New Directions. *Contemporary Educational Psychology*, 25(1):54–67.

Michael Sailer, Jan Ulrich Hense, Sarah Katharina Mayr, and Heinz Mandl. 2017. How gamification motivates: An experimental study of the effects of specific game design elements on psychological need satisfaction. *Computers in Human Behavior*, 69:371–380.

Michael Sailer and Lisa Homner. 2020. The Gamification of Learning: a Meta-analysis. *Educational Psychology Review*, 32(1):77–112.

Michael Sailer and Maximilian Sailer. 2021. Gamification of in-class activities in flipped classroom lectures. *British Journal of Educational Technology*, 52(1):75–90.

Katie Seaborn and Deborah I. Fels. 2015. Gamification in theory and action: A survey. *International Journal of Human-Computer Studies*, 74:14–31.

Hans van Halteren. 2002. Teaching NLP/CL through games. In *Proceedings of the ACL-02 Workshop on Effective tools and methodologies for teaching natural language processing and computational linguistics* -, volume 1, pages 1–9, Morristown, NJ, USA. Association for Computational Linguistics.

Maarten Vansteenkiste and Richard M. Ryan. 2013. On psychological growth and vulnerability: Basic psychological need satisfaction and need frustration as a unifying principle. *Journal of Psychotherapy Integration*, 23(3):263–280.

An educational Gamebook on computational linguistic methods for the development of taxonomies

Fritz Kliche[1] and **Ulrich Heid**[1] and **Ralf Knackstedt**[2] and **Thomas Klupp**[3]
[1]Institute of Information Science and Natural Language Processing
[2]Institute of Business Information Systems
[3]Institute of Creative Writing and Literary Studies
University of Hildesheim
{kliche, heid, ralf.knackstedt, kluppt}@uni-hildesheim.de

Abstract

We report on a course on computational linguistics and business information systems which includes different concepts of serious games. We developed an interactive Gamebook which features elements such as a contiguous story, quizzes and games. The story mirrors tasks of our students in a laboratory-like part of the course (problem-based learning). In several situations in the story, the readers are given choices for the continuation of the storyline. Based on individual choices, the protagonists in the Gamebook are successful or fail. Wrong decisions anticipate and prevent possible wrong or at least unhelpful decisions in the "real-world" laboratory tasks. We describe elements and concepts of the Gamebook and draw conclusions from an evaluation provided by the course participants.

1 Introduction

We report on an ongoing experimental course combining topics from computational linguistics and business information systems which includes serious games, a concept referring to stories, quizzes and games which should be fun and entertaining, but which also have an educational purpose (Bellotti et al., 2013).

The playful elements are offered in an interactive Gamebook which was written specifically for the course. It tells the story of three students attending a fictional university course which roughly covers the same topics as the real-world course. Next to the story, it includes quizzes and games on the contents from computational linguistics and business information systems which we want to convey.

Using the Gamebook, we first aim at a motivational effect provided by playful elements. Second, these elements build on reinforcing teaching strategies rooted in the long traditions of "Programmed Instruction" (e.g. Skinner, 1954 Calleder, 1969) and computer-assisted learning which are based on the idea that learners profit from immediate feedback.

Another central concept is problem-based learning. Following Boud and Feletti (1997, 2), this strategy does not start with the presentation of knowledge, but with a problem. Knowledge and skills are acquired by a sequence of "problems" which are embedded in a context, supplemented with learning materials and support from the lecturers.

In our course, instead of exercises coined for a specific learning unit, the participants work on a project from the field of business information systems, in order to understand computational linguistic techniques as tools for real-world problems. We are guided by the idea that this approach is similar to applications of NLP methods outside of a classroom situation. They would typically require decisions on appropriate text data and NLP tools, and include the possibility to fail with unsuitable strategies.

The overall goal from the business information systems perspective is the development of domain descriptions by means of taxonomies in the sense of Nickerson et al. (2013). They describe the objects of a given domain, their properties and relations in terms of dimensions, which are attributed with features. During the course – and in the Gamebook – we use a taxonomy on the topic of "carsharing" developed by Schoormann et al. (2017) as an exemplary use case. Table 1 shows three of its dimensions and some attributed features. Overall, this taxonomy has 16 dimensions and 82 features.

Section 2 refers to related work. In section 3, we detail the environment for which the Gamebook was written: The student public and the subject matters we taught. Section 4 reports on the Gamebook and its features. We describe the design for the evaluation of the Gamebook by the course participants in section 5. In section 6, we draw conclusions from the experiences using the Gamebook and the

Proceedings of the 1st Workshop on Teaching for NLP, pages 37–43
September 18, 2023.

Dimensions	Features
Vehicle classes	City car I Mid-size car I Van I ...
Customers	Private customer I Business customer I Public sector I ...
Propulsion	Electric I Combustion I Hybrid I ...

Table 1: Part of the taxonomy on carsharing developed by Schoormann et al. (2017).

evaluation and describe our lessons learnt.

2 Related Work

Playful elements were often applied for Natural Language Processing. Next to serious games or forms of gamification included in courses, applications also include e.g. games with a purpose (GWAP) which use gamified elements for motivating users to leverage human work intensive tasks such as linguistic annotations, e.g. word sense labeling (Venhuizen et al., 2013).

The Workshop series "Games and NLP" (cf. e.g. Madge, 2022 for the proceedings of the 9th edition) discusses games and gamification for Natural Language Processing.

Möslein-Tröppner and Bernhard (2018) focus on collaborative aspects of Gamebooks for education. They give best practices for storytelling and for the design of decision paths, e.g. for the structured integration of collaborative elements using flowcharts.

Benefits from gamified features are widely studied. An example of a study on gamified educational tools is provided by Mazarakis (2017). He develops an online quiz with 170 questions on geography and finds a motivational effect when participants acquire "badges" for correct answers, which are icons with e.g. a light bulb symbol, lettering such as "Godlike" or similar motivational content. We adopted this concept for the Gamebook.

Li et al. (2020) describe their experiences during an NLP course using problem-based learning approaches. The task during the course is to develop a text summarization system for a large collection of documents. They evaluated the course with five items on the students' self-assessments. The positive effects on motivation and problem solving ability in the context of the course's topics were higher for undergraduate students than for graduate students.

Motivational and hedonic qualities have also been seen as elements of the evaluation of software, with a focus on user experience and strategies to enhance the motivation of users to work with a given software, which we could use for our evaluation. E.g., Hassenzahl et al. (2000) investigate the importance of hedonic qualities (e.g., if a software is perceived as interesting), ergonomic qualities (such as ease of use) and the extent to which a software is evaluated as appealing.

3 Student public and teaching objectives

3.1 Student public

The Gamebook was written for a masters' course with 24 participants at the University of Hildesheim in the summer of 2023.

The course is taught in co-teaching between the business information systems institute and computational linguistics. Consequently, also the student public is diverse: Participants study programs in information systems development, information management, or translation studies and technical writing. Their prior knowledge of computational linguistics and of corpus-based methods is rather limited (maximally one or two BA courses). For this public, getting operational with corpus and NLP tools in a laboratory-like setup is a non-trivial task.

3.2 Teaching objectives

The basic idea underlying the course and the Gamebook is that the construction of taxonomies (in the sense of table 1) can be massively supported by computational linguistic tools. Learning objectives are thus (i) taxonomies as an element of information system design, (ii) the design of practical projects to develop a taxonomy by using computational linguistic tools, (iii) the principles underlying the tools and a critical evaluation of their output with a view to taxonomy building.

Following the example of carsharing, the participants of the course are asked to identify a subdomain of the domain of alternative forms of transportation, and to develop a taxonomy for the selected subfield.

The computational linguistic pipeline proposed for taxonomy building involves corpus design (selection of appropriate sources) and corpus development, linguistic annotation and corpus exploration. For the latter, not only pattern-based data extraction and querying are offered, but also tools based on BERT architectures (Devlin et al., 2019). Figure 1 depicts the pipeline.

More in detail, concepts of web crawling using the web crawler Trafilatura (Barbaresi, 2021), data cleansing and corpus building are introduced. We address lemmatization, part-of-speech tagging and underlying methods. The corpora are made available in the corpus analysis software CQPweb (Hardie, 2012). We integrate BERTopic (Grootendorst, 2022) for topic modeling and the related keyBERT (Grootendorst, 2020) for keyword extraction. Using a method according to Nickerson et al. (2013) the participants iteratively develop their taxonomies in groups of three students each.

4 The Gamebook

The Gamebook is given as an additional source of information for the students, next to standard materials (transparencies, sample data, notes on the principles underlying the tools, as well as on their use).

The Gamebook is divided into six thematic episodes of about 15 pages each, an introduction and an epilogue. It is given in PDF files and is currently implemented as ebook. Students are provided with a new episode every second week, synchronized with the program of the course. The Gamebook distinguished three types of textual elements:

(A) It contains the story which includes "choose your own adventure" elements: At several points in the storyline readers have to take decisions which impact on the remainder of the episode and in some cases on the overall success of the fictional student team.

(B) The Gamebook conveys subject-related content on computational linguistics and business information systems. This content is framed by the story, but can be read independently.

(C) The Gamebook contains several quizzes and games.

4.1 Story and decision points

The story is a typical hero's journey, including a quest, beginning in a lecture of a course at the beginning of the semester. The professor talks about the compilation of taxonomies, and announces that the best group of the course will win a voucher for one year of free carsharing. The story tells how the three protagonists follow the course, sometimes eager to win the competition, sometimes more interested in simply passing the course with little effort, and sometimes failing, depending on decisions of the readers.

While learners read the storyline, they are presented with choices. Depending on their decisions, different continuations of the story are offered (in different sections of the book). Thus, the story is individually adapted for each reader based on the knowledge and mastery of the contents to be learned. At the end of each episode, the different storylines meet again, in order to reduce the number of possible reading paths.

In several parts of the book, readers can collect various forms of points, which are relevant in the final episode: Depending on the results, the end of the story comes in six variants, ranging from a bad and disappointing performance of the three protagonists in their fictional university course, to the best of the possible ends where the fictional characters win the carsharing voucher.

An example for a scene with a decision point is situated at a car exhibition where the fictional students have to go through a sequence of tasks related to corpus exploration strategies, and where each task is waiting next to a given exhibit. The choice of exploration strategy (precision-oriented, providing relatively few examples, most of which are highly taxonomy-relevant vs. recall-oriented, providing much more results, but only a handful of which are relevant for the taxonomy) is connected, for the purpose of the story, with a decision whether a standard family car is to be visited next, or a fancy sports car.

When readers decide for the sports car, the story leads the fictional student group to the rather disappointing result of getting quite few taxonomy-relevant corpus examples, while the other path provides richer and more usable results. In either case, the fictional team verbalizes the reasons for the outcome, stating e.g. that the large amount of unspecific results was due to using the too general query. In some cases, the reader can even decide to go back to an earlier point in the sequence of analysis steps, and to try out an alternative path. Students reading the Gamebook may thus get access to best practice recommendations for their own

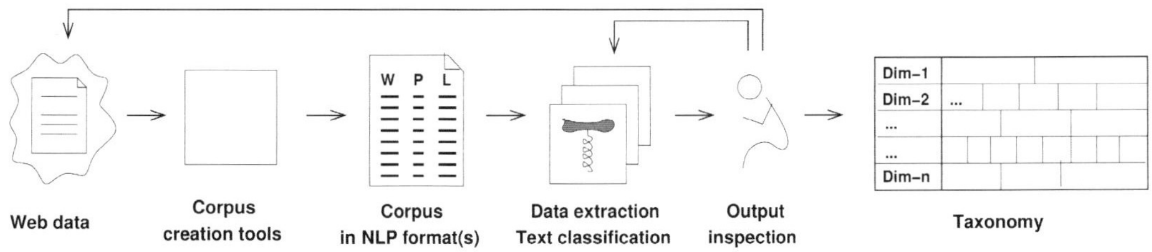

Figure 1: NLP pipeline for the development iterative definement of a taxonomy.

projects without having themselves to lose time in backtracking after avoidable mistakes or unhelpful steps of their work.

4.2 Subject-related content

Next to the story, the Gamebook embeds subject-related information. The following quote is an excerpt from the Gamebook and its English translation, giving an example for the embedding of information from the realm of business information systems, here the beginning of a definition of taxonomies.

> Du verkneifst dir eine Antwort und packst deine Sachen aus, der Prof schaltet indessen den Beamer ein. „Vor aller Praxis“, sagt er, „kommt aber die Theorie: Wie eigentlich erschließt man sich einen fremden Gegenstandsbereich wie zum Beispiel das Carsharing? Wie rückt man unbekannten Phänomenen auf den Leib?“ Er sieht erwartungsvoll in den Raum. Dein Sitznachbar – Ben, dieser Statistik-Ben, mit dem Du auch im Mensch-Maschine-Kurs sitzt – meldet sich. „Indem man eine Taxonomie entwickelt“, strebert er los. Der Prof nickt, dann deutet er auf das Whiteboard, auf das der Beamer jetzt einen Text projiziert: „Bitte, zur Einführung!“ Du wischst dir die nassen Haare aus der Stirn und liest:
>
> Taxonomien
>
> - Taxonomien sind Modelle, mit denen Wissen über Phänomene expliziert werden kann. Als Artefakte sind sie vom Menschen geschaffene Werkzeuge.
> - Sie dienen den Zwecken, Phänomene anhand von Dimensionen und Dimensionsausprägungen zu beschreiben, zu verstehen, zu analysieren und zu gestalten.

Translated into English:

> You refrain from answering and unpack your stuff, while the professor switches on the projector. "Before all practice," he says, "there is theory: How do you make an unfamiliar subject such as carsharing accessible? How do you get to grips with unknown phenomena?" He looks expectantly into the room. The person sitting next to you – Ben, that statistics Ben with whom you also sit in the human-machine course - raises his hand. "By developing a taxonomy," he nerds out. The professor agrees, then he points to the whiteboard onto which the projector is now displaying text: "Please, as an introduction!" You wipe your wet hair out of your forehead, and read:
>
> Taxonomies
>
> - Taxonomies are models that can be used to explicate knowledge about phenomena. As artifacts, they are man-made tools.
> - They serve to describe, understand, analyze and design phenomena by means of dimensions and features.

4.3 Quizzes and games

We use quizzes and games to allow student readers to test their knowledge of the fields discussed in the course and the decisions they would take in presence of certain kinds of data output from the computational linguistic tools.

As an example, figure 2 shows a part of a game on part-of-speech tagging. The readers have to move through a "board" with 6×6 fields.[1] Beginning on the "Start" field, they read the first of 11

[1] In the online version to be developed later in 2023, extra points can be earned by users who get through this parcours particularly quickly.

questions concerning the interpretation of part-of-speech tagging:

> Put your game token on the field *Start*. You see output from the part-of-speech tagger. You can reach each field adjacent to *Start*, also fields which are diagonally adjacent. One lemma in the example is wrong. Which one? Move your game token to the corresponding field.

As the sample sentence includes the expression "[erleichtert das] Autoteilen" ("[makes] carsharing [easier]"), the field with the example "Autoteil" is the right choice – as this lemma is wrong.

When readers find the correct field, its adjacent fields contain a correct answer for the second question:

> Please search for the underlying tagset online. Are tokenization, part-of-speech tag "KON" and lemma "bzw." correct for token *bzw.*?

The course participants read the Gamebook on their own. We discuss the episodes in the classroom, but it is not checked or controlled which strategies the students chose and which decisions they made while reading. Likewise, the quizzes and games are played individually, and the correct answers are given in the Gamebook itself.

5 Evaluation design and early results

We evaluate both the course and the Gamebook with a questionnaire which distinguishes three dimensions:

- One part of the questionnaire deals with the students' expectations and perceptions with respect to the contents and the form of both the course as a whole and the Gamebook. We ask for previous knowledge on the subjects, about the proportions of theoretical parts, practical exercises in the classroom and the time invested for the Gamebook. Concerning the Gamebook itself, we ask for options (5-step Likert scale) on items such as "I enjoy reading the texts" or "there should be more alternative storylines".

- We use 10 questions on students' expectations on self-efficacy, as proposed by Schwarzer and Jerusalem (1999, 15). E.g., the questionnaire asks how the participants evaluate their problem solving competence in the context of the course.

- We follow the User Experience Questionaire (UEQ) of Laugwitz et al. (2006) in the reduced form developed by Alberola et al. (2018) consisting of 11 questions. It measures the effectiveness and efficiency, but also the hedonic quality of software products.

A first round of student feedback has been collected in the seventh week of the course as a mid-term evaluation, a second round at the end of the course.

We asked in another text field for a mistake the participants would quite likely had made in their own practice work, had they not first read the Gamebook. Several answers mentioned problems with regard to web crawling. Web sites might not contain enough relevant text data, or the texts collected from the crawler might not be as relevant as expected. Also, the problem of duplicate text content in crawled texts was mentioned.

An interpretation of this feedback could be that the Gamebook is perceived as helpful for the laboratory work of the student groups, but less for theoretical background on computational linguistic methods.

Table 2 shows average results (scale 1-5) from some questions concerning the design of the Gamebook. The evaluation showed that students clearly preferred a realistic scenario (students attending a university class) over e.g. fantasy elements (average of 2.18 resp. 1.71).

The second item asks if the participants read alternative storylines. They indicate with average scores of 2.82 and 2.67 that they rather do not, possibly supporting the assumption that an extrinsic motivation dominates the occupation with the Gamebook.

On the other hand, the participants report that there should be more alternative storylines (average scores of 3.31 and 2.92) – possibly because the decision points were directly related to the tasks of the real-world student projects.

With an average score of 3.53 the students indicate that the Gamebook is rather supportive, and they evaluate it with average scores of 4.31 and 4.27 as creative. Finally, the Gamebook is perceived as rather well understandable (scores 3.82 and 3.71).

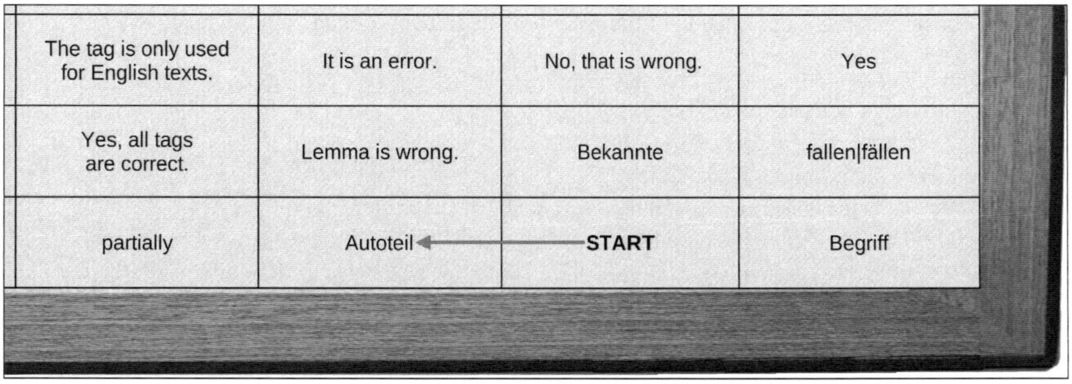

Figure 2: Example for C. Game on part-of-speech tagging.

Question	Average Score: Mid-term	Average Score: Final
Instead of the setting in a university, I would have liked a story featuring fantasy elements.	2.18	1.71
If there are alternative storylines, I read all of them.	2.82	2.67
There should be more alternative storylines.	3.31	2.92
How do you evaluate the Gamebook: $\pm$ supportive	3.53	3.50
How do you evaluate the Gamebook: $\pm$ creative	4.31	4.27
How do you evaluate the Gamebook from $\pm$ understandable	3.82	3.71

Table 2: Evaluation results referring to the design of the Gamebook.

6 Conclusions and lessons learnt

We presented the main components of a Gamebook addressed to a public of master students with little or no background in computational linguistics. The course where we use the Gamebook combines contents from information system design and from NLP. The Gamebook is intended to allow students to get a feeling for best practice use of NLP tools for taxonomy building without having to go through time-consuming and possibly off-putting experiences and mistakes in their own practical laboratory work. We also expect the Gamebook to be an element of motivation.

Based on our evaluation, we draw some first conclusions which might be valuable for similar projects. First, the Gamebook was evaluated as being creative and motivating. Second, we conclude that the story and the playful elements should not deviate too far from the objectives of the lecture. E.g., fantasy elements were not desired according to the evaluation, and elements of theoretical background which are not directly applicable to the students' projects are evaluated less favorably.

The students confirm that the Gamebook helped prevent pitfalls both with respect to taxonomy building (e.g. mistakes in the taxonomy such as overlapping or redundant dimensions and features) and to the use of corpus data (e.g. duplicate or corrupted content in the crawled text data). This confirms our main motivation for the development of a Gamebook.

The storyline of the Gamebook that follows the model of a quest for a treasure (Möslein-Tröppner and Bernhard, 2018) can be seen as a parable for courses in applied corpus linguistics (research question, corpus design and exploration, presentation of findings). We argue that parts of the fictional story are reusable in different contexts.

Our next steps will be to provide the Gamebook as an ebook made available via an OER portal[2]. Based on the evaluation results, we are interested

[2]www.twillo.de

in detailing the motivational factors of playful elements in both computational linguistics and business information systems, which seem to be most fruitful when they are directly connected to the extrinsic motivation of the course participants.

7 Acknowledgements

This work was carried out in the framework of the project "Development of taxonomies", financed by the Ministry of Science and the Arts of the German federal state of Lower Saxony, in the framework of its program "Innovation Plus" (project IP2021/P109).

References

Catherine Alberola, Götz Walter, and Henning Brau. 2018. Creation of a short version of the user experience questionnaire UEQ. *i-com*, 17(1):57–64.

Adrien Barbaresi. 2021. Trafilatura: A web scraping library and command-line tool for text discovery and extraction. In *Proceedings der ACL-IJCNLP 2021*, pages 122–131, Bangkok.

Francesco Bellotti, Bill Kapralos, Kiju Lee, Pablo Moreno-Ger, and Riccardo Berta. 2013. Assessment in and of serious games: An overview. *Advances in Human-Computer Interaction*.

David Boud and Grahame Feletti. 1997. Changing problem-based learning. introduction to the second edition. In *The challenge of problem-based learning*, pages 1–14, London. Kogan Page.

Patricia Calleder. 1969. *Programmed learning: Its development and structure*. Longman, London.

Jacob Devlin, Ming-Wei Chang, Kenton Lee, and Kristina Toutanova. 2019. BERT: Pre-training of deep bidirectional transformers for language understanding. In *Proceedings of the 2019 Conference of the North American Chapter of the Association for Computational Linguistics: Human Language Technologies*, pages 4171–4186, Minneapolis, Minnesota. Association for Computational Linguistics.

Maarten Grootendorst. 2020. KeyBERT: Minimal keyword extraction with BERT. DOI: https://doi.org/10.5281/zenodo.4461265.

Maarten Grootendorst. 2022. Neural topic modeling with a class-based TF-IDF procedure. arXiv:2203.05794.

Andrew Hardie. 2012. CQPweb: Combining power, flexibility and usability in a corpus analysis tool. *International Journal of Corpus Linguistics*, 17(3):380–409.

Marc Hassenzahl, Axel Platz, Michael Burmester, and Katrin Lehner. 2000. Hedonic and ergonomic quality aspect determine a software's appeal. In *Proceedings of the CHI 2000*, pages 201–208, The Hague.

Bettina Laugwitz, Martin Schrepp, and Theo Held. 2006. Konstruktion eines Fragebogens zur Messung der User Experience von Softwareprodukten. In *Mensch und Computer 2006*, pages 125–134, München. De Gruyter.

Liuqing Li, Jack Geissinger, William A. Ingram, and A. Fox, Edward. 2020. Teaching natural language processing through big data text summarization with problem-based learning. *Data and Information Management*, 1(1):18–43.

Chris Madge, editor. 2022. *Proceedings of the 9th Workshop on Games and Natural Language Processing within the 13th Language Resources and Evaluation Conference*. European Language Resources Association, Marseille, France.

Athanasios Mazarakis. 2017. Gamification: Eine experimentelle Untersuchung der Spielelemente Abzeichen und Story. In *Mensch und Computer 2017 – Tagungsband*, pages 3–14, Regensburg. Gesellschaft für Informatik e. V.

Bodo Möslein-Tröppner and Willi Bernhard. 2018. *Digitale Gamebooks in der Bildung: Spielerisch lehren und lernen mit interaktiven Stories*. Springer Gabler, Wiesbaden.

Robert C. Nickerson, Upkar Varshney, and Jan Muntermann. 2013. A method for taxonomy development and its application in information systems. *European Journal of Information Systems*, 22(3):336–359.

Thorsten Schoormann, Dennis Behrens, and Ralf Knackstedt. 2017. Carsharing Geschäftsmodelle: Entwicklung eines bausteinbasierten Modellierungsansatzes. In *Smart Service Engineering: Konzepte und Anwendungsszenarien für die digitale Transformation*, pages 303–325, Wiesbaden. Springer Fachmedien Wiesbaden.

Ralf Schwarzer and Matthias Jerusalem. 1999. *Skalen zur Erfassung von Lehrer- und Schülermerkmalen. Dokumentation der psychometrischen Verfahren im Rahmen der Wissenschaftlichen Begleitung des Modellversuchs Selbstwirksame Schulen*. Freie Universität Berlin, Berlin.

Burrhus F. Skinner. 1954. The science of learning and the art of teaching. *Harvard Educational Review*, 24(2):86–97.

Noortje Venhuizen, Valerio Basile, Kilian Evang, and Johan Bos. 2013. Gamification for word sense labeling. In *Proceedings of the 10th International Conference on Computational Semantics (IWCS 2013)*, pages 397–403, Potsdam, Germany.

Author Index